The Essence of the Gita

The Essence of the Gita

By
SWAMI SARADANANDA

Translated by
SWAMI TYAGANANDA

Sri Ramakrishna Math
Mylapore, Chennai 600 004

Published by
The President
Sri Ramakrishna Math
Mylapore, Chennai-4

II-2M 3C-12-2001
ISBN 81-7120-872-X

Printed in India at
Sri Ramakrishna Math Printing Press
Mylapore, Chennai-4

Preface

SWAMI VIVEKANANDA once described the Bhagavad Gita as the great poem which is "the crown jewel of all Indian literature. It is a kind of commentary on the Vedas." Today not many have the patience, time or opportunity to read the entire Vedas. The Gita is more accessible. It is easy to understand the Gita if it is learnt from someone who has realized the truth of its teachings through spiritual discipline and struggle.

Swami Saradananda, an eminent disciple of Sri Ramakrishna, was such a person. Six of his Bengali talks on the Gita, published in the book *Gita-tattva*, present a brilliant summary of the Gita's teachings. What we have in these talks is the essence of the Gita; if we can grasp the essence properly, our study of the complete text of the Gita will be more fruitful.

The *Gita-tattva*, published by the Udbodhan Office in Calcutta, has in all fifteen Bengali talks given by Swami Saradananda: the first six of these deal exclusively with the Gita and the rest deal with other Vedantic themes. The six talks on the Gita which comprise this book were translated in the *Vedanta Kesari* from January 1985 through February 1986 by Swami Tyagananda. He was the editor

(1987–1997) of *Vedanta Kesari,* a monthly journal of the Ramakrishna Order, published from Sri Ramakrishna Math, Chennai. At present, he is the Assistant Minister of the Ramakrishna Vedanta Society, Boston, USA. He has thoroughly revised the translation for this book edition, which we are releasing for wider circulation. May the Gita continue to inspire seekers of truth everywhere.

Chennai, 29 January 2000
Swami Vivekananda Jayanti

Translator's Note

SWAMI SARADANANDA, an eminent disciple of Sri Ramakrishna, gave this set of six talks to a predominantly youthful audience. Five of these talks were given between 6 December 1902 and 31 January 1903; the last talk was given at the Harisabha in Bally on 13 January 1904. The talks, all extempore, were full of insights vital for a healthy spiritual growth.

This translation from the Bengali original follows the text faithfully. The paragraphs in the translation are smaller and a few subheadings have been introduced for the benefit of the reader.

In his talks Swami Saradananda frequently quoted the Sanskrit verses from the Gita. In this book the Sanskrit portions appear as footnotes and their translation has been indented in the body of the text. In most places the translation from Sanskrit is Swami Saradananda's own. It is not always literal, but is meant to express the essence of the verse quoted by him. In a few places the swami quotes only the Sanskrit verse and follows it up with his comments. In such cases the translator has provided a simple English rendering. All references in parenthesis, unless otherwise stated, refer to the Gita.

S.T.

Contents

1
Introduction

The Gita is held in high esteem in India because it contains the essence of Hinduism. In the hymn "The Glory of the Gita" *(Gita Mahatmya)*, there is a beautiful verse:

> The Upanishads are cows. Sri Krishna is milking these cows. Arjuna is the calf. The wise drink this milk, the great Gita-nectar.[1]

All the Upanishads are like cows. Sri Krishna milks these cows and Arjuna is a calf. Just as a cow gives milk only when her calf comes near her, Sri Krishna's teaching—the "Gita milk"—becomes available only as a result of Arjuna's questions. For whom is this milk meant? For those who are wise. Those who have read a few books and can speak eloquently are these days considered wise. But the Gita says that those who merely indulge in talk are not wise. Only those who have come face to face with truth are wise. Such people have had the direct realization of the Self through transcendental knowledge. Those who can distinguish the Real from the unreal are wise. It is said that a special variety of swan exists who can

---

1. सर्वोपनिषदो गावो दोग्धा गोपालनन्दनः ।
   पार्थो वत्सः सुधीर्भोक्ता दुग्धं गीतामृतं महत् ॥

1

drink the milk alone from a mixture of milk and water. In the same way, in this world there is a mixture of the Real and the unreal. The wise discard the unreal and hold on to the Real. Only such people can understand—and make others understand—the Gita.

Sri Krishna's Life, the Best Commentary on the Gita

People have interpreted the Gita in various ways. In India teachers from three traditions have explained the Gita from their own points of view. Sri Sankaracharya, the teacher of nondualism *(advaita)*, has written his commentary on the Gita with a nondualistic interpretation. Similarly, Sri Ramanuja, the teacher of qualified nondualism *(viśiṣṭādvaita)*, and Sri Madhva of the dualistic *(dvaita)* school, have interpreted the Gita justifying their own philosophical outlook. It is not necessary for you to study all those commentaries. Your minds are not yet influenced by any particular philosophy and they are, so to speak, still fresh. It is enough to understand the meaning as it reveals itself to you spontaneously.

Whenever the meaning does not become clear by itself, we can use another method. Those who have read the *Mahabharata* will understand that the life of Sri Krishna is itself the best commentary on the Gita. The teachings of the Gita find resonance in everything that Krishna did in his own life. Take for instance the instruction to remember always one's true nature as the immortal and indestructible Self (ātman) in spite of the apparent identification with the body. Or the teaching which asks us to do our duty without considering our own gain or loss. Or the teaching to remain unperturbed by the momentary ups and downs of life. We see that Krishna practised all of these. So if we are not able to understand any teaching in the Gita, we can study the life of Sri Krishna and through that we will understand the correct meaning.

The Gita, though small, contains all the ideas regarding the spiritual Self (ātman), God (īsvara), the embodied Self (jīva) and the world (jagat), that are recorded in the Upanishadic portions of the Vedas. In some places the very language of the Upanishads is used. It is for this reason that the Gita is considered an Upanishad. Another name for it is "Gitopanishad."

The hymn "The Glory of the Gita" mentions the benefit of studying the Gita. It says in one place: "One who reads the Gita regularly gets a human body even in the next birth."[2] The Gita student is not born in any inferior species. Don't think that getting a human birth is very easy! It is quite difficult. But when we get it, we become eligible to get also the

_____

2. गीताध्यायसमायुक्तो मृतो मानुषतां व्रजेत् ।

strength of knowledge, the strength of devotion or any other strength. Sri Sankaracharya says:

> Only through God's grace can we have these three things that are difficult to get: human birth, the desire for spiritual freedom, and the company of a great soul.[3]

Without the grace of God it is not possible to have these three things together. First, a human birth, second, the desire for spiritual freedom: this involves disregarding both physical and mental pleasures and keeping a high ideal fixed in one's life. If there is a steady, unchanging ideal, it will in course of time lead us to God. Most people are busy with sensual delights. How many, indeed, live with a higher ideal in life?

The third rare thing is the company of a great soul: to have the company of someone whose life is built upon the highest ideal and to learn from him or her the purpose of human life. Why is this so rare? All of you talk about religion and spirituality, and so do I. But why is it not effective? Our words lack force because they don't come from the heart. Our thoughts and words are at variance. Our minds yearn for worldly enjoyments and yet we mouth words of renunciation. How, then, can our words be effective? But take the case of someone whose life is built upon a high ideal and whose thoughts and words are

---

3. दुर्लभं त्रयमेवैतद्देवानुग्रहहेतुकम् ।
मनुष्यत्वं मुमुक्षुत्वं महापुरुषसंश्रयः ॥

in harmony. Every word of this person opens, as it were, the door within and cuts the fetters of ignorance *(maya)*. The words of such great souls carry a special power. How irresistible were the words of Sri Ramakrishna! Read the words of Christ and Buddha. Although they are now hundreds of years old, how powerful they are even today! But if you and I speak those very words, they will hardly cause a ripple in anyone's mind.

If we are able to build our lives upon a high ideal, then our words also will increase in power. Then whatever we say will touch the hearts of people. Whatever we try to make powerful, will increase in power. If we try to enhance the power of the mind, our mental power will increase. In the same way, if we try to improve the power of speech, our capacity to discuss some theme will increase.

According to Vedanta, this world is the creation of the mind. The mind's power is awesome! Even the materialists in the West accept this. History also reveals the fantastic power of the mind. Marie Antoinette, the Queen of France, was known for her beauty. The people of Paris revolted one day, put her and the King in jail, and decided to send them to the guillotine the following day. Next morning it was seen that all the hair on the Queen's head had turned white! The intense night-long worry had transformed her into an old hag by the next day. Such is the power of the mind! If the mind wants anything intensely, it will certainly get it. We are not able to desire anything with all of our mind, so we don't get it.

The mind, Sri Ramakrishna used to say, is like a bag of mustard seeds. Once the seeds fall out of the bag, it is impossible to gather them all again. They all spread out under the furniture in the house or in the crevices of the walls. Try as we may, we will never be able to gather all the seeds. In the same way the mind too gets dispersed. Some of it is attracted to beauty, some of it to taste, a part of it to wealth, name and fame and so on. It then becomes impossible to fully gather in the mind. That was why Sri Ramakrishna loved young people: their minds were one-pointed. The seed of spirituality strikes roots immediately in such minds.

Every chapter of the Gita is called a yoga. Yoga means to join or to unite. It is a way to unite ourselves with God. The first chapter is called the "Yoga of Despondency" (viṣāda yoga). Why is despondency a yoga? Because the despondency of Arjuna was instrumental in taking him toward God. Hence the name "Yoga of Despondency." In the same way, the other chapters of the Gita have names such as the "Yoga of Knowledge" (sāṁkhya yoga), the "Yoga of Work" (karma yoga), the "Yoga of Renunciation" (sannyāsa yoga), and so on.

Some may say that the Gita was taught only to Arjuna. What significance can it have for us? None of us are going to take part in any war. Nor do we ordinary people have anything in common with the great warrior Arjuna. How can the teaching given to such a great student be of any benefit to us?

In answer it could be said that although Arjuna was much superior to us, he was also a human being. We too are human beings. Just as he was deluded at times, we too are deluded often. Like him, we too are called upon to face many obstacles and calamities in our quest for truth. Like him again, we too are in the midst of both inner and outer warfare. That is why the study of the Gita holds a message for us, gives us peace of mind, and offers solution to the problems of life. Thanks to the study of the Gita, those who had lost their way have shed tears of repentance and have changed their entire life-course and directed it toward high ideals.

Is the Gita an Interpolation?

There is one more point to be considered. Has the Gita been grafted onto the body of the *Mahabharata*? Some Western scholars feel that the Gita is an interpolation. Many Indians too swallow that opinion. They say that no historical records of ancient India exist. They never did exist! So it is too unreasonable to accept that such a lofty philosophy was actually taught before the war at Kurukshetra began. Before believing in something, should we not try to find out whether the thing was even possible?

The only reply to this is: Let them become as old as India. Then we shall see how much of history they are able to preserve. How ancient is India! How many revolutions have swept over it! How often has destruction taken place here, only to be followed by reconstruction! What will the West understand? It was born just the other day. We see the West discovering ideas today which were discovered in India ages ago. This is sufficient to know what great heights India had scaled at one time. Where in the world existed the universal acceptance as in India? Our scriptures tell us that one may take lessons even from a person of low birth, because knowledge is God, and so it is divine. Wherever there is knowledge, there is the seed of wisdom. Strive for knowledge from the wise. The Gita (4.37) says, "The fire of knowledge reduces all karma to ashes."[4] It destroys all impurities. Sri Ramakrishna used to say, "Once a person tastes sugarcandy syrup, will he care any more for the syrup of molasses?"

Religion and philosophy are the very life force of India. They have sunk deep into the bones and vitals of the people of this country. Every activity of the people here resonates with this life force. Until we have any conclusive evidence to show that the Gita's teachings could not have been given before the war,

---

4. ज्ञानाग्निः सर्वकर्माणि भस्मसात् कुरुते तथा ।

why should we reject our ancient national belief and accept these modern views?

The message of the Gita was delivered by Sri Krishna, a divine incarnation. What may be impossible for ordinary people like you and me is certainly possible for great souls like him. This also has to be taken into account. Besides, we do not see any deviation in the language of the Gita from the other parts of the *Mahabharata*. How then can we agree with these modern scholars? Those who have lived in holy company know that a holy person remains unaffected by what we consider hard knocks in life and, in the midst of these, gives the highest teaching. This we have actually seen. Sri Ramakrishna was suffering from a terrible disease and was almost without food for six months. But all those who were with him were flooded with great joy. He filled their hearts with bliss by sharing with them his own spiritual practices and helping them find answers to the intricate questions of life. He was totally unaffected by disease, sorrow or pain. Arjuna was in the company of an incarnation of God. How long, indeed, would it take for him to teach Arjuna! So the Gita is not an interpolation.

You may say that the Gita holds for us a spiritual meaning. It is this: "In life we have to fight innumerable wars day and night. There is, for instance, the fight with the senses or the fight for subsistence. We have no respite and no peace. The

Gita show us how we can win these wars and fulfil the real purpose of life." Very well! If you want to believe this, go ahead. There is no difficulty.

Every Verse of the Gita Is a Mantra

I said that the Gita enjoys the same status as the Upanishads. There are many who read at least a chapter of the Gita every day after their bath. They consider every verse of the Gita as sacred as a mantra. The Gita too, like a mantra, has its particular seer *(ṛṣi)*, deity *(devatā)*, Vedic metre *(chanda)*, and seed *(bīja)*.

The seer of the Gita is Vedavyasa, because he had "seen" these mantras. He saw the truth and then composed it in verse for the benefit of all. The mantras were first revealed to him. So the "seer" in this case means the same as what we call "author". The "deity" is the main theme of the mantra and the "Vedic metre" is the specific arrangement of words in which the mantra is recorded.

Just as a tree comes from a seed, every scripture has a particular theme, supporting which or elaborating on which, the scripture is composed. What is the "seed" or the theme of the Gita?

You have been mourning for those who should not be mourned for. Yet you speak words of wisdom. (2.11)[5]

5. अशोच्यान्वशोचस्त्वं प्रज्ञावादांश्च भाषसे ।

This means that you speak one thing and in your heart of hearts believe something else. In other words, you are not straightforward. Those whose speech and thought are at variance have to suffer. They have a long way to go before they attain God-realization. Sri Ramakrishna used to say that an important spiritual practice is to make speech and thought identical. The Gita too teaches us that. Straightforwardness alone is the seed of the mighty tree of righteousness (*dharma*).

Every mantra has a particular power source (*śakti*). The power source of the Gita is embedded in this verse:

> Giving up all duties, take refuge in Me alone. I will liberate you from all sins, grieve not. (18.66)[6]

How many plans we make— "I shall do this," "I shall do that"! But often all our plans come to naught at one stroke. Some great unseen power shatters them to pieces. We are, as it were, mere puppets in its hands, doing everything at its will. But this should not lead us to imagine that we have no free will of our own. We are kind of caught between free-will and fate. It is a peculiar situation. It is something like semi-darkness or semi-light. We can consider it as light or we can consider it as darkness. But we can't just say that it is one and not the other.

---

6. सर्वधर्मान्परित्यज्य मामेकं शरणं व्रज ।
   अहं त्वा सर्वपापेभ्यो मोक्षयिष्यामि मा शुचः ॥

From the beginning of creation we have been trying to understand this transcendental principle. Every thinker in the West, beginning from Socrates, has tried to find answers to questions such as "What is this world? From what source has it manifested? Is it autonomous or governed by someone else?" But none of the thinkers have been able to make any headway because it is not possible to get answers to these questions through the mind. The mind has its limits. How can a finite entity know the Infinite? How can the mind answer the questions which cannot be answered unless one transcends the mind and the senses?

There is a beautiful story which illustrates this idea. A scholar tried for a long time to understand and teach all these transcendental principles. Frustrated at his utter failure, he went to the seashore to drown himself. There he saw a small boy engrossed in an unusual kind of play. He had made a small hole in the sand and was bringing water in his tiny palms to fill the hole. He was trying very hard and was spending considerable time running back and forth. This sight caught the scholar's attention and he became curious to know exactly what the child was doing. Going near, the scholar asked, "What are you doing, son?" The boy replied, "I am bringing all the water from the sea into this hole." The scholar couldn't suppress his smile. But at once the thought came to his mind, "Am I not doing something similar to this myself—trying to know through the mind the principle that transcends the mind?"

Swami Vivekananda used to say, "All of us are ready with our measuring rods. We want to understand God after trimming Him down to a manageable size!" No, that is not possible. The mind is material. The ancient sages knew that the mind, which is made of subtle matter, is controlling gross matter. But the mind has no power of its own. It derives its power from the spiritual Self, which in fact controls everything. In the West many believe that the mind itself is the Self. That is not true.

The Gita says that to know the answers to all these questions, one must be first of all a fit student (adhikari). How can one become a fit student? By harmonizing one's own mind and one's own will with the Cosmic Mind and the Cosmic Will. The thoughts and vibrations of one must tally with the thoughts and vibrations of the other. Then the hurdles to knowledge, produced by desires, are removed from the mind and a special power becomes manifest in it. For this reason the way of life taught by the Gita is embodied in this verse: "Giving up all duties, take refuge in Me alone." (18.66)

"God is the controller of the universe. Let my will be one with His. I desire nothing else." Those who firmly cling to this idea live in tune with the Great Power. They alone are able to efface their egos and attain to supreme knowledge.

But most of the time we harbour in our minds just the opposite idea. Instead of being in tune with the Cosmic Will, we dig our own graves in pursuit of our desires. Have you noticed this? All of us know that change is the law of life and yet we all struggle to preserve our temporary bodies eternally! Don't we commit the same mistake in our affections also? We want to hold on to the body and mind of the beloved. We want to possess for all time the impermanent body and mind of the beloved. That is why our so-called love produces attachment. *Real* love is a part of God. It doesn't make us attached. Genuine love gives infinite freedom to the beloved, without any claims of possession. But people become enslaved by their desires and, against the Cosmic Will, want to possess temporary objects permanently. Keep this in mind.

This reminds me of a tale from Aesop. A poor old man was one day trudging along with great difficulty with a pile of firewood on his head. It was summer, the load was heavy, and the strength of the old man was failing. After going some distance he got tired and sank down, his body perspiring. Then he began cursing his fate, saying, "Alas! Has even death forsaken me?" No sooner had he said these words than the fierce form of Death appeared before him and said, "Old man! Did you call me?" In his heart of hearts, the man wanted to live. So in a faltering voice, he stammered, "Sir, this load is very heavy.

I am unable to lift it up by myself. So I called you to help me with it!" Our case too is similar to this when we are called upon to give up the transient things of the world.

Arjuna at Kurukshetra

The beginning of the Gita is very beautiful. There are two parties, all set to fight, with great warriors on either side. Every one of them has a special conch shell. In those days, a warrior could be identified by the sound of his conch. The sound of the conches fills the air. Now Arjuna requests Krishna, "Please park my chariot between the two armies. Let me see who is going to fight with me." Until this point no weakness has assailed Arjuna. He is full of courage. Sri Krishna maneuvers the chariot as directed. Arjuna sees in the opposing army his grandfather Bhishma, who had been given the boon to die at the time of his choice. He sees also his teacher Drona, who had taught him the science of warfare. Arjuna also sees Karna and Kripacharya besides many other brave warriors.

According to some commentators, after seeing all this Arjuna became somewhat afraid. He was not ignorant of Bhishma's boon and he knew of Bhishma's victory over Parasurama in battle. He also knew of the valour of Karna and the special boon Lord Siva had bestowed on Jayadratha, the prince of Sindhu. So it is no wonder that Arjuna became diffident.

The critics give another proof for Arjuna's fear. In the eleventh chapter of the Gita (11.26), when Arjuna sees the Cosmic Form *(viśvarūpa)* of God, he particularly takes notice of the death of Drona, Bhishma, Jayadratha and Karna. Only after that vision does Arjuna know that he is destined to emerge victorious in the battle. He also realizes whose power is really at the back of all that is taking place and comes to know of other things that are to follow.

A question may be raised: After hearing the entire Gita, Arjuna calmly indulges in the gruesome massacre at Kurukshetra. What does this show— his religious nature or its opposite? The Gita thus appears to be merely a collection of instigating utterances to make Arjuna participate in the war. It appears that Sri Krishna does not even hesitate to make untruth appear as truth to incite Arjuna in this barbarous killing of his relatives. Can killing human beings, particularly one's own relations, be under any circumstances a noble deed?

In reply it may be said that if the intention is noble, killing others may lead to truth, righteousness and success. It is the intention that determines whether a thing is right or wrong. Take the case of killing in a war for the defence of one's country or the execution of a pernicious sex offender to stop the molestation of women. These are good acts though they involve killing of others. For the defence of Chittore, the women cut off their hair to provide bow-strings to kill the enemy. Although these women were motivated by the desire to kill others, we nevertheless feel a spontaneous urge to worship them as goddesses, don't we? But if others are killed for one's own pleasure, the mind of the killer goes down to the level of a cruel beast. That is why "small" and "big", or "good" and "bad," are qualities not inherent in any work. These are determined by the intention of the doer.

Wonderful indeed is the mind's capacity! Three or four types of feelings, even if they are mutually contradictory, can arise simultaneously in the human mind and we are not aware of it. That is what happened to Arjuna. He became confused at the thought of killing Drona, Bhishma and his kith and kin in the battle. This happened due to love as well as the fear of defeat. Perhaps only the thought of victory did not strike him. Attachment produces confusion and that, in turn, often leads to weakness, deflecting a person from the path of duty and truth. Prior to the battle, Arjuna stood for truth, not selfishness. He wanted to have a peaceful settlement by having only five villages. How much he tried to avoid the clash! Only when he realized that avoiding the battle would encourage injustice, impropriety and evil, did he get ready to fight for the cause of truth. To eliminate oppression is the duty of a person who belongs the class of warriors *(kṣatriya)*.

Wherever you see injustice and oppression, you must oppose it. Everyone in the world is interconnected. If you are hurt, I too am hurt. Suppose you see me being oppressed by somebody and you keep silent. You say to yourself, "That's OK. *I* haven't been oppressed. Why should I bother about what happens to someone else?" You are clearly in a deluded state. You should realize that along with me you also have been oppressed. The nobility of your mind has been attacked. Blinded by selfishness, you have today refrained from opposing injustice. When you are oppressed tomorrow, you will not have the strength to retaliate. In this way a person gradually marches along the road to degradation and slavery.

Arjuna became confused on the battlefield. "No, I don't need happiness," he said. "If all the near and dear ones die, then what shall I do with the kingdom?" Sri Krishna saw that Arjuna was unconsciously hiding his inner fear and had forgotten the purpose of his life. Arjuna had begun to think that he was fighting for his own interests. He had forgotten that it was his duty to take up arms for the cause of truth and to counter the oppression of others. On earlier occasions—such as at the time of the demon Baka's killing—whenever the Pandavas had seen injustice and impropriety, they had fought it as a matter of duty. Here Arjuna had forgotten all that.

He thought that he had taken up arms to win the kingdom.

This is what happens to us in life. Blinded by beauty and the lure of wealth, we often lose sight of the goal. If we are practising spiritual disciplines (*sadhana*), we may be able to recover the forgotten goal. But without it, everything comes to naught.

Sri Krishna's Rousing Call

Seeing Arjuna's condition, Sri Krishna imparts his special teaching in these two verses:

> O Arjuna, from where has this delusion of yours come? How could this delusion come upon a great person such as you, obstructing your march to heaven? O Arjuna, give up this faint-heartedness. This kind of mental weakness is unbecoming to a strong person such as yourself. Shake it off. Arise and fight. (2.2-3)[7]

We learn something important from this. Whatever produces delusion and weakness is sinful. What is true of the mind is also true of the body. Any activity that leads to physical weakness is also sinful. Today children are so busy with passing their academic examinations that they neglect their health. We do not realize that this is a type of sin.

---

7. कुतस्त्वा कश्मलमिदं विषमे समुपस्थितम् ।
   अनार्यजुष्टमस्वर्ग्यमकीर्तिकरमर्जुन ॥
   क्लैब्यं मास्म गमः पार्थ नैतत्त्वय्युपपद्यते ।
   क्षुद्रं हृदयदौर्बल्यं त्यक्त्वोत्तिष्ठ परन्तप ॥

Once young people leave college, they hardly have
any health to boast of. They are unable to do
anything worth-while with their limbs. The result is
inefficiency in most of their work. It is essential
to take care of one's health. Weakness is the result
if we neglect health. We cannot escape the conse-
quences of abusing the body and the mind.

Arjuna then says, "How can I possibly fight
with Bhishma? How can I kill my teacher Drona?"
But he soon realizes that these noble words are not
corroborated by the thoughts in his mind. The mind
understands you see! Arjuna says:

> I am overpowered by my own commiseration. My state is
> indeed pitiable. The mind has lost its tenacity. I am
> distraught and thoroughly confused. Have compassion on
> me. I pray to you and beg you: I am your disciple, please
> teach me. (2.7)[8]

Now Sri Krishna speaks, pinpointing the source
of Arjuna's confusion:

> You speak like a wise person but you are grieving over
> something the wise do not grieve for. (2.11)[9]

These words of Sri Krishna come as a blow to
Arjuna. What do the wise say? What is eternal? The

---

8. कार्पण्यदोषोपहतस्वभाव:
   पृच्छामि त्वां धर्मसंमूढचेता: ।
   यच्छ्रेय: स्यान्निश्चितं ब्रूहि तन्मे
   शिष्यस्तेऽहं शाधि मां त्वां प्रपन्नम् ॥

9. अशोच्यान्वशोचस्त्वं प्रज्ञावादांश्च भाषसे ।

body, after all, is ever-changing. The wise never grieve over this ephemeral body. But Arjuna was grieving over it. So his words and mind were not in agreement with each other. He was not wise.

Two Important Laws of Spiritual Life

We learn two important and essential laws of spiritual life from these words of Sri Krishna. First, don't give in to weakness of any kind. Weakness is a great obstacle to the attainment of the goal. Secondly, we should harmonize our thoughts with our words. If we are able to practise these two teachings in our lives, the doors of success will open wide. To whatever extent we follow these two laws, to that extent will we—wherever we may be, either in worldly life or out of it—achieve something tangible in life.

2

Jnana Yoga – I

In the last class we learnt in particular about two things.[1] First, whatever produces weakness, physical or mental, is sin. It must be given up fully, because under its influence we are overcome by delusion and forget the words of the scriptures and the spiritual teacher. The second thing we learnt was that there should be harmony between our thoughts and our speech. Which means, it won't do to talk like a wise person and act in a contrary manner. Sri Ramakrishna used to say that harmonizing one's thoughts and speech is the chief spiritual practice. This is true in every situation and is essential everywhere—in matters religious as well as secular. Many may say that harmonizing thoughts and speech may be possible in religious life, but it cannot be practised in secular life. But that is not true. With the advances made in various fields in this modern age, people now realize that even in a very secular endeavour such as trade, the extent of their dynamism and hard work done with thoughts and speech in harmony, determines the degree of their success.

---

1. Chapter 1

There is another thing we ought to know about the Gita. Sri Krishna taught the Gita to Arjuna on a battlefield. The question is: *who* heard the teachings and *who* wrote them down? Neither Vyasa nor Sanjaya were present on the battlefield. From the study of the Gita we know that King Dhritarashtra's attendant Sanjaya related the Gita to his master and the great sage Vyasa wrote it in a verse-form in his *Mahabharata*. How did they come to know? Dhritarashtra, according to the story, was blind. When he prayed to the great sage Vedavyāsa to let him know the details of the battle at Kurukshetra, the sage wanted to give him divine eyes *(divya-dṛṣṭi)*. But he did not accept it. Then in order to fulfil his desire, the sage Vyasa gave yogic eyes to Sanjaya. That was how Sanjaya could see what was happening on the battlefield and was able to relate it to Dhritarashtra.

Why the Gita Begins with Self-Knowledge

Today we shall deal with Jnana Yoga. When we are overcome by delusion, nothing but Self-knowledge can take us back to the right path. When someone close to us passes away or when a terrible whirlpool makes a sudden appearance in the stream of our life, uprooting in a stroke all our aspirations, we can keep our balance in such moments of trial only if we have Self-knowledge. Transformations have occurred, or will occur, in the lives of all. In Arjuna's life this great battle brought about the transformation. Attaining Self-knowledge under the guidance of Sri Krishna, Arjuna overcame this great crisis in his life easily and was able to uplift himself. But there have indeed been many who have lost their way in similar circumstances, degrading themselves and plunging into the jaws of death! That is why the Gita begins with the teaching on Self-knowledge. This teaching is not only for Arjuna but for people of all nations and all times. That is why Sri Ramakrishna also said, "Get a firm hold over the knowledge of nonduality and then do as you like!"

Everything in this world keeps changing. This law binds every material thing. Who can say why and in which direction everything is moving? The evolutionists claim that a gradual progress is taking place. But they can't say *why* it is taking place. From a seed evolve the tree, the flowers and the fruits. Why? For what purpose? This question has always risen in the human mind in the past as well as in the present. But so far it has not been answered. The scholars in the West feel that the purpose of all this is to establish a well-organized and healthy society. In India the scriptures say that this mysterious, cosmic chain of creation, preservation and destruction is without beginning.

In God's eyes this world is merely a purposeless play *(līla)*. If we say that God wished to fulfil some purpose by creating the world, we would also attribute imperfection to Him. So the sages say that this creation is merely God's sport. He remains unchanged even after creation. But from our point of view, if we try to understand why we struggle in this world, it appears that the purpose behind it is to snap the bonds of relative existence *(samsāra)* and to attain Self-knowledge. The purpose is to attain perfection and to go beyond all misery and suffering. It may also be said that a society would be ideal in every respect were it composed of those who were masters of their senses, people who had attained Self-knowledge. Such an ideal society would always have peace and bliss, as the inner deficiencies of all its members would have been totally eliminated.

The Body, the Mind, and the Self

When Sri Krishna saw that the delusion of Arjuna would not leave him until he had Self-knowledge, he said:

It is not that you or I did not exist in the past or will cease to exist in the future. (2. 12)[2]

The Self is ageless and immortal; the body is material. Whatever is born of matter has to abide by the laws of matter. Whatever is born of subtle matter, i.e. the mind, has to abide by the laws of subtle

---

2. न त्वेवाहं जातु नासं न त्वं नेमे जनाधिपाः ।

matter. It is futile to try holding on eternally to a material thing. By its very nature, matter is prone to change. It is ignorance and foolishness to think, "I won't allow matter to change. I shall keep it in the same condition eternally." This is what people always try to do in the world. Once Yudhishthira was asked, "What is the greatest wonder in the world?" He replied:

> We see people leaving everyday for the abode of Death
> and yet those remaining behind aspire to live eternally.
> What, indeed, can be a greater wonder than this?[3]

We see people dying every day. There is no one in the world who has not known someone who died. Yet all move about as if they were immortal. Everyone has this inherent desire to hold on eternally to the material body.

Everything material passes through these six states: origination, subsistence, growth, transformation, decay and destruction. The scriptures say that even the mind is material: it is made of subtle matter. Many Western scholars say that "mind," "spirit" and "soul" mean the same thing. In India the Charvakas too held that opinion. The mind or the Self is but a product of the brain, they said. It is produced and destroyed along with the brain. Some evolutionists say that the mind is not just a product of the brain

---

3. अहन्यहनि भूतानि गच्छन्ति यममन्दिरम् ।
   शेषाः स्थिरत्वमिच्छन्ति किमाश्चर्यमतः परम् ॥

but an independent entity. It is what constantly produces the feeling of I-ness and that itself is the Self. But it is our common experience that mental strength has its ups and downs. The mind therefore is changeful like matter. How then can it be the Self? So the scriptures say that the Self is an independent entity which gets its work done through the mind, just as it does through the body.

A question may be asked: "Malfunctioning of the mind leads to insanity. If indeed the Self is independent of the mind, how is it affected by the changes in the body and the mind? Why do they make the Self appear different?" The answer is that the Self never undergoes any change. The change we see is due to some other cause. For instance, suppose someone is playing a violin and all of a sudden the string snaps and the music stops. Now, where is the fault—in the violin player or in the violin? Similarly, the Self has created the body-mind instrument to experience the world full of forms, tastes, smells, etc. When the instrument goes out of order, it is useless. Though the instrument doesn't work as before due to its breakdown, the Self, who plays the instrument, remains unaffected. In this way our scriptures have shown the distinction between the body-mind and the Self. The body-mind is matter, the Self is of the nature of consciousness or knowledge. The mind too, like the body, has birth, sustenance and destruction. The Self is eternal and indestructible.

> The Self is changeless, all-pervading, unmoving, immovable and eternal. (2.24)[4]

> As childhood, youth and old age are to the body of the embodied soul, so also is the attaining of another body upon death. Just as the body is subject to changes like growth, maturity and decay, death also is one of these changes. (2.13)[5]

The scriptures further say that we can become directly aware of this through yoga.

The Self is changeless. A question may be asked: Who then experiences all this? Who becomes happy and miserable? The Vedas say that the Self is the experiencer only as long as it is identified with the senses and the mind. When its identification ceases, it at once realizes its true nature. Our identification with the mind and the senses is what the scriptures call the causal body, because if we had not forgotten our true nature and identified ourselves with the body and mind, neither ignorance nor misery nor death could have touched us. This forgetfulness is the cause of all mischief and hence it is the *causal* body. Knowledge alone—and nothing else—can destroy this causal body.

But even forgetfulness of its own intrinsic nature does not make the Self subject to growth and decay. It is ever-perfect. Can merely the feeling of

---

4. नित्यः सर्वगतः स्थाणुरचलोऽयं सनातनः ।

5. देहिनोऽस्मिन् यथा देहे कौमारं यौवनं जरा ।
   तथा देहान्तरप्राप्तिर्धीरस्तत्र न मुह्यति ॥

identification with the mind and the senses ever make any real change in the Self? No, it remains as it always is. As Sri Ramakrishna used to say, let a piece of phosphorus remain in water even for four hundred years. Remove it and strike, and see the fire! The Self too is like that. No sooner does it understand the body and the mind to be a bondage than the Self immediately discards them and realizes its own nature.

We are seeing this dream called the world. We see a variety of dreams. I may, for instance, see myself as dead, as if someone has sliced my body in two, a stream of blood is flowing and in it are lying my severed head and torso. And no sooner do I wake up than I see that it was all nothing! The dream is broken. In the same way, all of us will wake up one day from the dream of this world. That is why Yaska[6] says that every one has an equal right to Self-knowledge, be he or she a noble person *(āryan)*, a barbarian *(mleccha)*, a priest *(brāhmana)*, or a labourer *(sūdra)*. Give the teaching to everyone. Who knows whose Self will be "awakened" and when! Sri Ramakrishna used to say that if there is intense detachment, Self-knowledge can be attained within three years, or three months, or even three days. The Gita says:

---

6. Yaska (c. 600 BCE), a Sanskrit scholar, was the author of Nirukta, a work on etymology, which discusses and interprets difficult Vedic words.

At the time of death, even a momentary rise of that
Knowledge can destroy all ignorance and result in unity
with Brahman. (2.72)[7]

Beware of Distorted Teachings

Self-knowledge is the mainstay of the Vedas.
This is the only national wealth of India. It is from
India that this knowledge spread to the other parts of
the world. The day that India discards this knowledge will be the day she is destroyed. It will take a
long time for people in other parts of the world to
appreciate and attain this knowledge. In the field
of spirituality India is still the teacher of the world.
Accept the British and others as your teachers in
the fields of commerce, politics, warfare and other
subjects, and learn from them. But they have not
become fit yet to occupy the same place in the field of
spirituality. What more foolishness can there be than
to set aside the living embodiments of spirituality
such as Sri Ramakrishna and others, and go to these
foreigners professing other religions to hear the glory
of their faith![8]

These days some sects have adopted in their own
distorted way a few principles of the Vedic religion
and are preaching it as the "real" religion. Some say,

---

7. स्थित्वास्यामन्तकालेऽपि ब्रह्मनिर्वाणमृच्छति ।

8. Christian missionaries had unleashed an aggressive campaign of
proselytization of the Hindus at the time these classes were given.

for instance, that after ten million births a person will attain Self-knowledge and will be liberated, whether the person wants it or not. Such a doctrine of karma is nothing but arrant fatalism. Nowhere have the Vedas taught thus. The Vedas say that we can be free this very moment if we want or we may continue dreaming for an infinite period if we so choose. At no place in the Vedas is mentioned any fixed time for a person's spiritual liberation. Even the Puranas merely say that we get a human birth after 8.4 million births in other bodies. How indeed can there be any specific deadline for a person's spiritual liberation? Birth and death never really affect the Self. The Self is as if asleep. When it awakes, it will be free. The Self is the support of all cosmic energy. The day it realizes this, the day it realizes that it is the "king's son," it would return "home" and remain immersed in its own glory.[9]

Some sects claim that they are in contact with liberated souls residing in the snow-bound Himalayas. They are always able to see these people, touch them and even receive letters from them! Well, if it is true, be it so. But since neither the Vedas nor the Puranas nor other scriptures make even a

---

9. The reference is to a story often told in the Vedanta tradition. A prince was kidnapped immediately after birth and was left in a forest, where he was brought up by a tribal couple. He grew up thinking of himself as a tribal. Years later the king's men found him, told him of his real identity and brought him to his real home.

passing reference to them, it is not necessary for us to busy ourselves with them. Life is short. Where is the time to bother about every thing that others may say?

Karma and Rebirth

The Self is unaffected by joy and sorrow. It is perfect. But the body is subject to change according to the laws of the material world. Now a question may be raised: What happens when a person dies? The gross body, through which the mind works, becomes worn out. The Self discards this emaciated body and acquires a new one, just as a person throws away a torn dress and wears a new one. All the impressions *(samskāras)* of the thoughts, efforts and work done through the body remain in the mind. The mind, the intellect, the ten sense organs and the impressions of sense experiences make up the subtle body of the Self. The subtle body is made of subtle matter. It does not die along with the gross body. It remains associated with the Self even after death. In other words, even after discarding the gross body, the awareness that "I have a body and senses" is not destroyed.

Impelled by the impressions of the earlier body, the Self then desires to acquire or create another gross body. It becomes attracted to the parents who will be able to provide it with a body suitable for the development of its impressions. Its past actions themselves propel it towards its would-be parents. The subtle body has neither length nor breadth nor weight. It begins to reside in the mother's womb right from the time of conception. The subtle body is not visible to the eye, but is material nonetheless. It is more subtle than even space and air. Through the new gross body, the Self resumes its quest from where it had left off at the death of the old body and continues to gain knowledge.

From what has been said so far, it is easy to understand why all of us are not born with the same intellectual capacity. Or why the mind and body of each person is dissimilar from those of every other person. Or why there exist natural differences in our mental and spiritual lives. The theory of rebirth alone can explain this. Western scholars try to explain away these obvious differences by saying that the child derives its qualities—good and bad—from its parents. There is no doubt that to a large extent the child inherits various diseases and mental characteristics from its parents. When the child is in no respect similar to its parents, they try to ascribe it to the differences in education. In this way the parents and the teachers are burdened with the sole responsibility. These scholars can offer no other solution to explain the individual differences among people.

The Vedanta scriptures say that these differences are due to karma, our past actions. Whenever we perform any action, it is done with a purpose. In order to achieve that purpose, we activate the forces within us and around us in a particular way. Once all these forces are awakened and activated, they cannot but produce certain changes as a result. These changes are experienced or considered by us as good or bad, joyful or sorrowful. If experienced as good or joyful, the mind wants to hold on to the changes for all time. On the other hand, if the changes are experienced as bad or sorrowful, or those which would surely bring sorrow in the future, then the mind tries to get rid of them by all possible means. In this way our work produces joy or sorrow and also leads to *more* work, just as from a seed springs forth a tree which in turn produces flowers, fruits, and *more* seeds. It is clear that this life is not sufficient to experience the results of all our work in the form of joy and sorrow. These effects are thus experienced in the next birth.

Vedanta divides all our karma into five groups: the obligatory *(nitya)*, the forthcoming *(āgāmi)*, the accumulated *(sancita)*, the activated *(prārabdha)*, and the prohibited *(pratiṣiddha)*. Obligatory karma like ablutions and twilight devotions *(sandhyā-vandana)* should be done daily. One doesn't get any special result by doing them, but their neglect causes demerit. The scriptures prohibit stealing, killing and other such things—these are called prohibited karma. The accumulated karma is that which we did in our earlier births but have not as yet reaped its results. Some of it is being exhausted in the present life: we experience this karma in the form of a healthy or unhealthy body and mind as well as in our life's various struggles. This is called activated karma. Forthcoming karma is that which is done in this life or that which will be the cause of our next birth.

In one of his books Sri Sankaracharya gives a beautiful example to explain these three types of karma—the forthcoming, the accumulated and the activated. Suppose a man is shooting arrows with the help of a bow. One arrow has already been shot, another has been mounted on the bow with the intention of shooting, and many other arrows are on his back in the quiver. The arrow that has been shot will strike, come what may, the object at which the arrow was aimed. This can be compared to activated karma, which is beyond human control. The body and mind will certainly experience the effects of this karma. There is no way of escaping the effects, however much we may want to do so. That is why liberated souls experience the effects of activated karma even after attaining Self-knowledge. The arrow which is about to be shot may be compared to forthcoming karma. Just as we may, if we wish, not shoot this arrow, the effects of the forthcoming karma we can avoid if we wish. The arrows remaining in the quiver can be compared to accumulated karma.

The scriptures say that we must reap the results of whatever karma we do. Moreover, one karma leads to other karma: in this way the bondage of karma continues to increase day after day and life after life. When will it end? Only when Self-knowledge is attained. The bondage will disappear when we realize that we are the indivisible, indestructible, ageless, deathless and infinitely blissful Self. Never has the Self suffered and never will it suffer. It is the body and the mind that are working and suffering. Their "nearness" to the Self—or the Self's identification with the body and the mind—makes it appear as if the Self is doing things and suffering. It is like the nearness of the hibiscus flower which makes the crystal appear red. It is not the original colour of the crystal. And yet it is only the presence of the ever-pure Self that makes any work possible. That is why after the dawn of Self-knowledge, all karma becomes impotent and comes to an end. The fire of knowledge reduces them all to ashes.

All work in its entirety attains its consummation in knowledge. (4. 33)[10]

The fire of knowledge reduces all karma to ashes. (4. 37)[11]

---

10. सर्वं कर्माखिलं पार्थ ज्ञाने परिसमाप्यते ।

11. ज्ञानाग्निः कर्वकर्माणि भस्मसात् कुरुते तथा ।

Self-Knowledge, the Goal of Life

The goal of our life is to attain Self-knowledge. The goal can be defined in terms of neither joy nor sorrow. A person may be married or a monastic, a student or a business person, no matter who or where a person is, it is possible for us to work always in such a way that every work will nudge us forward on the path to Self-knowledge. It is simply not possible to separate religion from our daily life, though people may want to do so.

As if to make this clear, the teachings of the Gita are given on a battlefield, in the midst of the roaring currents of violence and hatred. There is not a moment to lose by remaining unprepared. All the brutal instincts of the human mind are shamelessly out to fight. If the highest teaching and practice of religion are possible there, is there any spot in the world where they wouldn't be? Who wants a religion that is not for all? The scriptures do not wish that one section of people should live in happiness and peace and the others suffer in toil and misery. True religion can be practised everywhere and by all, the monastic as well as the married. Religion takes all toward one goal. Religion says: "O child, you are truly infinite by nature. You may think that you are insignificant, someone having a body and experiencing joys and sorrows and destined to die. Yet even now you are what you really are and you will always remain that !" Listen to these words:

> Whoever thinks that the Self kills or whoever imagines that the Self is killed—neither of them knows the Self. The Self is neither born nor does it die. (2. 19)[12]

> [The Self] is never born and never does it die. (2. 20)[13]

> Whoever knows the Self to be eternal, whom will such a person want to kill? By whom, indeed, can this person be killed? (2. 21)[14]

Those who have attained Self-knowledge really do nothing. It is only their bodies and minds which continue to work automatically until their death. Good work and charity become natural to them.

We have seen that Self-knowledge takes us beyond joy and sorrow. So when someone becomes helpless due to sorrow and delusion, there is no other way than to make the person attain Self-knowledge. Without that even Arjuna could not shake off his sorrow and delusion. None can be freed from sorrow, delusion and weakness born of ignorance without seeing the Cosmic Form (viśvarūpa) of God and knowing oneself to be only an instrument in the hands of the Cosmic Power. Only when Arjuna saw that no one

---

12. य एनं वेत्ति हन्तारं यश्चैनं मन्यते हतम् ।
    उभौ तौ न विजानीतो नायं हन्ति न हन्यते ॥

13. न जायते म्रियते वा कदाचित् ।

14. वेदाविनाशिनं नित्यं य एनमजमव्ययम् ।
    कथं स पुरुष: पार्थ कं घातयति हन्ति कम् ॥

could do anything on one's own did he realize his error. Only then did Arjuna's sorrow and delusion vanish.

In the second chapter of the Gita, Sri Krishna not only taught Self-knowledge, he also tried to persuade Arjuna in an ordinary way. Sri Krishna told him, "You'll lose your reputation. People will call you a coward and insult you. It is better to die rather than to face all this." Failing to realize the value of this, people often become critical and say, "What rubbish has Sri Krishna spoken here! Do we have to do even evil deeds out of fear of public criticism?" No, it does not mean that. If we try to understand properly, we shall see that even these words of Krishna have deep import.

We see that those who are adored by people have some special quality in them. If they have no quality worth the name, the adoration of the masses doesn't last long. Good work always elicits praise from people in general, though they may not understand clearly the worker's noble attitude behind it. Even illiterate, ignorant people can judge for themselves the good and bad qualities of a person. This is because God dwells in all beings, and it is due to His power that every person has the natural capacity to distinguish between good and evil. If people revile us, it is for two reasons: either we are too evolved to be understood by people or we really deserve the censure. So we ought to know ourselves first. Only after we have examined ourselves minutely should we disregard the opinion of others. So Krishna showed Arjuna at the very outset that it was delusion which had produced his fear and this was why he was trying to run from the battlefield. If people were to condemn Arjuna, it wouldn't be without a just cause. Knowing this, Arjuna should rid himself of delusion. Sri Krishna then says:

> Even if you accept that the Self undergoes periodic births and deaths, you ought not to grieve. (2. 26)[15]

We will die one day. We all know that. From the very day a child is born, it starts moving toward death. So Krishna says, what is the use of worrying over the inevitable? This body is sure to go. We will get another one. Why then grieve over it? Only fools will lose sleep over this matter.

> No one knows from where we have come and no one knows where we shall go. All these worldly relations are only temporary. Why then do you grieve unnecessarily? (2. 28)[16]

If you know every being to be truly the immortal Self, then it is certain that no one will ever "die". Why then this grief?

---

15. अथ चैनं नित्यजातं नित्यं वा मन्यसे मृतम् ।
    तथापि त्वं महाबाहो नैनं शोचितुमर्हसि ॥
16. अव्यक्तादीनि भूतानि व्यक्तमध्यानि भारत ।
    अव्यक्तनिधनान्येव तत्र का परिदेवना ॥

Some look upon the Self with wonder, some speak of its nature with wonder, some hear of it with wonder, and some unfortunate ones there are who do not understand even after hearing of it. (2. 29)[17]

You belong to the class of warriors. If you lose the war, heaven awaits you for doing your duty on the battlefield. If you succeed, you win the kingdom. So arise and fight. (2. 37)[18]

And how will you fight?

Fight with equanimity, looking with evenness upon joy and misery, victory and defeat, gain and loss. (2. 38)[19]

If we do this, no sin can touch us. We don't have to bother about anything else. We only need to see that we are doing our work as a matter of duty and for the cause of truth. If we can work in the world with this attitude, if we can keep these thoughts always in our minds, if we can go on working like servants of God without calculating our own personal gain or loss, in no way can we remain in bondage. We shall gradually advance toward our spiritual liberation. This is the central theme of Jnana Yoga.

<hr>

17. आश्चर्यवत्पश्यति कश्चिदेन-
        माश्चर्यवद्वदति तथैव चान्यः ।
    आश्चर्यवच्चैनमन्यः शृणोति
        श्रुत्वाप्येनं वेद न चैव कश्चित् ॥

18. हतो वा प्राप्स्यसि स्वर्गं जित्वा वा भोक्ष्यसे महीम् ।
    तस्मादुत्तिष्ठ कौन्तेय युद्धाय कृतनिश्चयः ॥

19. सुखदुःखे समे कृत्वा लाभालाभौ जयाजयौ ।

3

Jnana Yoga – II

I have already said that the Gita is not an interpolation and there is also proof that it is not an interpolation. The study of scriptures shows us that Indian philosophers had one rare quality. If the modern philosophers in India and abroad develop this quality to some extent, it would greatly benefit not only them but also other people. Our ancient philosophers were never content to establish an idea only intellectually. They made efforts to translate the idea into practical life. After doing that successfully, they would share the truth with other people. When we study the life of Sri Krishna, we see that he himself verified by actual practice the truth of his teachings in the Gita. We see in his own life all the truths taught in the Gita thoroughly put into practice for the first time. So there is no doubt that it was he who taught the Gita.

What is Yoga?

We have seen something about yoga already. Yoga is to wholly direct the powers of the mind upon a specific object. We see a boy unable to study and pass the examination in spite of his efforts. What is the reason for this? He is not able to gather his mental powers in one place. A portion of his mind is always diverted toward different things. He is not able to focus his mind fully on any one object. The mental power is dissipated on other matters. Because of this he is unable to master the desired thing. Yoga is the easy way to reach or attain the goal, whatever the goal may be. And what is that easy way? It is to gather together all the powers of the body and mind, and focus them on the goal—be it wealth or spirituality or any work for the welfare of others. The easy way to do this task can in general be called "yoga."

From where will come the power to collect together the whole mind? All power is within us because the Self is the source of all power. The body, the mind and the intellect are only instruments of the Self. Using these instruments, the Self is playing, as it were, a great game. Just as efficiency is lowered when the instrument goes out of order, the play of the Self too is affected when the mind and the intellect become impure. It is then not able to manifest its infinite power. If, however, the mind and the intellect are pure with a preponderance of serenity *(sattva)*, the power inherent in the Self can manifest wonderfully.

What is Jnana Yoga?

Although the word "yoga" can be used in an ordinary way, the Indian scriptures use it only in connection with religion. Let us see now what Jnana Yoga is. Sri Ramakrishna used to say, "Knowledge leads to unity; ignorance, to diversity." When can we say that we have acquired *true* knowledge of something? It is only when we are able to see the light of that knowledge in all places and in all things. Those who have acquired the knowledge of music are able to detect the play of music in all sounds. They can understand and describe the pitch and varying strains of music in all sounds—be it the sound of a thing falling or the sound of a running vehicle or the sound of a person speaking. What is more, they can see the various "forms" of the different sounds. They perceive the play of music even in the play of colours. The whole of creation is to them a unique set of musical vibrations. They see sound as Brahman, the ultimate cause of the universe. Pythagoras used to hear wonderful music in the movements of the sun and the moon. He used to call it the "music of the spheres." Sri Ramakrishna used to hear the sound Om pervading the entire universe. He heard it in the chirping of birds, in the flowing of the river and in the tumultuous waves of the sea. He experienced the unstruck *(anāhata)* sound flowing through all sounds, in all places and at all times.

As in the case of music, so is it in the case of other subjects. Those who have acquired the knowledge of form or taste see the entire universe as only a modification of form or taste. Everyone has the knowledge of diversity and everyone experiences joy and sorrow. Even the things that appear to our gross eyes as inanimate show themselves to have life and some sort of knowledge by reacting to every blow they receive. The knowledge of things such as food, sleep and fear is equally present in animals, birds and humans. This knowledge is not what we are speaking of. But if we see the manifestation of one power or the operation of one law in certain diverse objects, then *that* is what we call knowledge.

A ripe fruit falls down from a tree, a stone which has been tossed up falls down to the ground, a person doesn't continue to rise in space by jumping up— so long as we do not perceive these facts as manifestations of one force, they do not help us much on the path of knowledge. But no sooner do we understand that it is all due to one force called gravitation than our knowledge increases rapidly. We are able to collect diverse phenomena into one stream. This is too well known to need elaboration. This kind of classification of different things and experiences into separate groups is called knowledge.

All these innumerable separate groups can be further classified into a smaller number of groups. The scriptures say that those who are able to see *all* these groups included in just one group are truly wise people. Once this truth is experienced, never again can ignorance come. So the Gita says that the person who sees always the manifestation of the One

everywhere is truly wise. Those who are able to see
the One in the many conquer death and go beyond joy
and sorrow.

Sri Krishna's life and teachings focus on this
central theme—how we can reach the One with the
help of knowledge. What does it matter *who* that
One is? From whoever all this universe has sprung is
that One and we have to go to the One. Call the One
by any name—God *(Īśvara)*, the Divine *(Bhagavān)*,
the Divine Mother *(Kālī)* or the All-pervading
(Brahman). The One is neither masculine nor
feminine nor even neuter.

How do we attain to the knowledge of the One?
Sri Ramakrishna used to say that if we are able to
apply all the powers of the mind to any pursuit, with
no thought of self-interest, then we shall certainly
attain the knowledge of the One. Whether we direct
our minds to God or to the world, if we can do that in
a perfect manner, then we shall see the manifestation
of that One. If someone can become mad as it were,
for the sake of one's country by giving oneself entirely
for its cause, then that One will be manifested in that
person through his or her patriotism. The study of
science or music or sculpture—it may be whatever—
if done with a fully concentrated mind, that in itself
will lead to knowledge of the One. This is the
teaching of Sri Ramakrishna. This teaching is new
and wonderfully true! It is as easy to hear as it is
difficult to practise.

We see that this is true of all things. That which is very easy can also be quite difficult. That which is very near can be, at the same time, quite far. We make a frantic search for the necklace which is around our neck. Such things often happen. The Self too, like the necklace, is so near that we are not aware of it. We do not believe that God is within us. To encounter the Divine we wander about everywhere, even on mountains and in forests. We undertake fasts. And when at last we are exhausted by the search, we discover that God is within us.

Sri Ramakrishna used to say that the human mind is like a bird perched on the mast of a ship. Once a bird was sitting on the mast of a ship. The ship set sail and went far out into the sea. Bored with sitting in one place, the bird flew off to go elsewhere. It saw nothing but water everywhere. It flew for a long time in all directions but was unable to find any place to land. Exhausted at last, it returned to the mast of the ship and sat down. In precisely the same way, the human mind also becomes fatigued after its search in different objects and in different places. At last it finds peace when it sees the One within.

Who Can Practise Jnana Yoga?

Although potentially present in everyone, the knowledge of the One is easily accessible to a pure intellect *(buddhi)*. It cannot be accessed by the

unrefined intellect of the worldly. The discipline
of Jnana Yoga and its application in daily life is
difficult. Only those with a pure intellect can do it.
We become fit students to practise Jnana Yoga only
when we can immediately put into practice whatever
our deep thinking convinces us to be right. An idea
arises in the mind, "I shall become a celebrity. I shall
acquire nationwide fame and honour." Then maybe
we give this idea some thought and find that it is
better to strive for God-realization than for name and
fame in this evanescent life. But if we are unable
to control the mind and run after worthless things
like wealth and fame, then Jnana Yoga cannot be
practised. In that case we must realize that our path
is different.

A student of Jnana Yoga needs to have the mind
perfectly under control. The mind must be totally
subjugated so that it obeys her or his commands
to the letter. When Jesus fasted for forty days to
manifest the latent divine power within him, Satan
came to tempt him. He promised to give him wealth,
fame, a kingdom, beautiful women and so on. Hearing
that, Jesus immediately said, "Get thee behind me,
Satan!" Away with you, you desire in the form of the
devil!

Within us also such desires are always rising.
The desires of our numerous lives come bubbling up.
Furthermore, when we set ourselves to work for the
common good with the best of intentions, hundreds of

desires arise all at once, like the descendants of the demon Raktabija, and torment us.[1] Only a person with all the senses under perfect control can perceive these seeds of desires and drive them away. But if the impressions *(saṁskāras)* are very strong, they cannot be driven away merely through reasoning. For such people the path is different. If the impressions are less strong, then it is possible to keep the mind under control through introspection. One who practises Jnana Yoga must have desires which are not so powerful that the mind cannot easily control them and keep itself steady.

Intense Rest in the Midst of Intense Activity

At every step in Sri Krishna's life we can see that he possessed the highest knowledge. Even during life's most critical moments, what remarkable steadiness and oceanic calmness he had! In any kind of situation Sri Krishna was completely unflappable, unwavering and unperturbed. We can see him in beautiful Vrindaban filled with flowers and fruits. Or in Mathura, surrounded by enemies. Or in

---

1. The reference is to the demon named Raktabija in the *Devi Mahatmyam* (commonly referred to as the *Chandi*) (8. 40-63). Every drop of blood that fell from his body during the fight with the Goddess produced another demon of his stature. Thus thousands of demons were produced when he encountered the Goddess in the fight.

Hastinapur, adored by the royal household. Or in the battlefield, saturated with love and hatred. Or in Prabhasa, resounding with past memories. Or even at the time of his own Yadu clan's destruction. Even before the destruction occurred, he sensed that it was the inevitable result of the law of cause and effect; the Yadus' karma itself produced the horrible result. When it could not be averted despite all effort, the illumined teacher of the Gita calmly witnessed the death of his clan. Although the destruction occurred before his very eyes, his mind remained unshaken and calm. Swami Vivekananda used to say that, according to the Gita, the ideal is to experience "intense rest in the midst of intense activity."[2] This is how a yogi lives.

Swamiji had the desire to have a portrait made of this scene of the Gita: Swamiji visualized Sri Krishna dressed as a charioteer, driving the chariot in the battlefield with his hands holding the reins. At the point where he hears Arjuna's sorrowful refusal to fight, Sri Krishna keeps the powerful horse under his control by pulling the reins with one hand. Krishna then turns his face towards Arjuna. In spite of the physical strain involved with keeping the horse in check, Sri Krishna's face bears the signs of a yogi because of his infinite inner calmness. Swamiji had

---

2. *The Complete Works of Swami Vivekananda*, 9 vols. (Calcutta: Advaita Ashrama, 1977), 1: 442, 476.

a great desire to have a painting which would depict Sri Krishna's amazing calmness even in the midst of the fierce Kurukshetra war.[3]

Nothing was certain at this time: no one knew how many kings would die, who would be victorious and who would lose. All were agitated and frenzied except Sri Krishna, who remained steady, calm and unshaken. He continued to work for the welfare of others and to restore moral values while simultaneously giving profound teachings on yoga.

This kind of calmness should be cultivated by all. A kind of intoxication enters into us when we work. That is bad. We lose command of ourselves. It is work that goads us on and it is the senses that drive us on. The boss surrenders at the feet of the servant and the puffed-up servant treats the boss any way he likes!

In the battle of daily life and at the workplace, we should always be calm. That is why the teachings of the Gita are not only for monastics. Nor are they only for the married. They are relevant to *all* people of *all* nations and for *all* times. That is why another name for the Gita is the "Gitopanishad". The special characteristic of the wisdom and teachings of the Upanishads is their universality. After showing different paths suitable to the various types of students, the sages of the Upanishads proclaim

3. *The Complete Works of Swami Vivekananda*, (1972), 7: 272-73.

boldly, "You are heirs to immortality. Immortality is your nature. Through delusion you may imagine yourself to be a noble person, a barbarian, a priest or a labourer. But none of these identities can bind you. You are free, you are free. You are *eternally* free." Only after seeing the Gita's universal spirit did the author of the "Glory of the Gita" *(Gītā Māhātmya)* declare that the Gita was produced by churning the Upanishads.

We have to cultivate a yogi's calmness in the intoxicating battle of life. We must learn to protect ourselves from the reaction which inevitably follows every work we do. Then alone will we be capable of doing something really great and be fit to be called human beings. It is not necessary to explain how often the intoxication of desire-propelled work leads to painful results. How many people sink to the depths of misery because of loss in trade and commerce and are unable to rise again! There are children who destroy their health in their maddened struggle to pass some test. Time and again we even see students commit suicide when they are not able to pass an examination in spite of their best efforts.

It is essential for all—particularly for those with secular responsibilities—to learn how to bring calmness in the midst of the intoxication of work. For these people the only means of progress in all matters, secular and spiritual, is work and work alone. There is no need to imagine that we shall lose our enthusiasm for work if we learn how to work calmly; this is proven by Sri Krishna's life.

Compare the teachings of the Gita with Sri Krishna's entire life and you will see not one iota of discrepancy. Although he never worked for himself, his enthusiasm for work surpassed the enthusiasm of all others put together. See him while playing in Vrindaban; see him in the royal courts of Mathura and Dwaraka; see him at the time of the Yadus' destruction; see him on the battlefield of the Kauravas and the Pandavas; everywhere we see in his heart an extraordinary calmness and peace *along with* tremendous enthusiasm for work.

It is said that Sri Krishna gave to Duryodhana eleven units[4] of his army before the battle started. Duryodhana thought, "I could not get Sri Krishna on my side. Well, what does it matter? His energy cannot equal the energy of eleven army units!" But just the opposite proved true in the battlefield. Sri Krishna's energy and perseverance, his infinitely resourceful power in moments of crisis, his fiery and energizing words in the darkness of utter despondency, and his uncommon cheerfulness and tranquil mind in the

---

4. The army unit referred to here is called *akṣauhiṇi* in Sanskrit. It consists of 21,870 chariots, with an equal number of elephants, three times as many cavalry and five times as many infantry. The total strength of the two armies was eighteen *akṣauhiṇis* or about 4 million men in all.

shadow of death and in the midst of the defeat of his own people—all these qualities made him as powerful as all the great warriors from both sides put together, what to speak of eleven of his own army units!

The Characteristics of an Illumined Person

The central idea of Jnana Yoga is this: Spiritual practice consists of negating—"not this," "not this" (neti neti).[5] We have to give up once and for all everything that stands as a hurdle on the path to the One. Hearing the teachings on Jnana Yoga, Arjuna asked, "What are the characteristics of one who has attained knowledge, the person of steady wisdom (sthitaprajña)?" Arjuna wanted to know the lifestyle and the habits of a person who has been able to keep his or her life steady in the strong current of cause and effect. How does the life of this person express itself through his or her words, habits and dealings with others? The Gita and other scriptures have recorded for our benefit the ways in which the enlightened ones have worked in this world.

It may be asked, "How can we learn anything by observing their behaviour? We are ordinary people full of lust and greed. We have dull intellects and we

5. This practice consists of disidentifying oneself from everything that is not one's true Self. When everything that is non-Self is negated, the person experiences his or her true Self as divine, free and immortal.

also desire the fruits of our actions. Unlike these great souls, we have no high ideal in life." This may be true, but unless we can fill our life with their kind of high idealism, detachment and unselfish enthusiasm, do we have any hope of progress? Moreover, many of us who are trying to lead purposeful lives under the guidance of a teacher often get caught in the whirlpool of activity and are unable to decide what we should do. Or we are assailed with doubts about the authenticity of the new ideas and experiences that we acquired on our spiritual path. We can be freed from all doubts and misgivings when, learning humbly from these world teachers, we are able to tally our own experiences with those of these great ones. We then recover our own peace of mind. That is why the scriptures ask students to observe carefully the characteristics of realized souls and try to cultivate them in their own lives. This is really our main spiritual practice.

The scriptures also ask us to remember that the authenticity of our spiritual experiences is confirmed if they tally with the teachings received from the scriptures and the spiritual teacher. Sukadeva was said to have been born with supreme knowledge. Even then, until he was able to tally his own realization with what he had learnt from the scriptures and his teacher, he occasionally fell into spells of doubt about the genuineness of his spiritual experiences. He asked his father, the great sage Vyasa, how to dispel his doubts. The father realized that some other arrangement had to be made since Suka's doubts had not been removed despite the fact that he had given the boy instructions from his very childhood. After much thought, he told Suka to go to the sage-king Janaka and accept him as his teacher so he could learn from him. When Suka went to Janaka's place, he had to wait at the door for seven days. No one seemed to be interested in him. In spite of this insult, no anger or hatred rose in Suka's mind. Then the sage-king welcomed him into the palace and offered him warm hospitality with great respect. Even with this kind of honour Suka did not forget the purpose of his visit. Janaka then explained to him the characteristics of supreme knowledge. When Suka was able to tally his realization with the teaching of Janaka and the scriptures learnt from his own father, then all his doubts were dispelled and his mind was at peace.

Let us see now what the Gita says about the characteristics of an illumined person.

An illumined person is one who has found inner content-
ment after giving up all desires, who has brought under
control lust, anger and other passions, and who is able to
to work using the sense organs without being controlled
by them. (2. 55)[6]

6. प्रजहाति यदा कामान् कर्वान् पार्थ मनोगतान् ।
   आत्मन्येवात्मना तुष्टः स्थितप्रज्ञस्तदोच्यते ॥

The illumined sages, like all of us, use their sense organs in order to work, but unlike us, they never forget the goal. They are always aware that the senses are their servants and they the masters. It is this fact that we forget; we are pulled wherever the senses drag us. One of the Upanishads says that the Self is the master riding a chariot. The body is the chariot; the senses are its horses and the mind their reins. The intellect, with the reins in hand, is the charioteer who is guiding the horses on the path full of sense objects. The destination is knowledge and peace. If the charioteer remains levelheaded because of good training, he or she can maneuver those mad horses properly even on a dangerous road. Otherwise the horses disregard the reins and go by any path they like, at times even toppling the chariot upside down. The pure intellect directs the horses properly to the destination. But the impure intellect, bound by desire and greed, surrenders to the horses and advances on the path to total destruction.[7]

Another characteristic of the illumined is that they remain serene in both joy and sorrow. In contrast, we are selfish and mad for our own personal pleasures. Even a little sorrow throws us off the balance. Taking the trouble to help strangers is out of the question—we remain carefree even if our neighbour is afflicted by the plague. Look at the

7. *Kathopanisad*, 1.3.3-9.

numerous famines we have in India. What are we doing about it? If this were to happen anywhere in the West, the whole country would have been agitated. People would have said, "Why should there be such famines? Why should millions die in our country for want of food?" They would have dedicated their lives to eliminate the problem. In these matters we Indians are inactive. We are full of inertia *(tamas)*. In practical life we are utterly lazy. Someone wrote recently that the number of Indians who have died because of famines in the last nineteen years is four times those who have died in wars throughout the world in the last 107 years. How awful!

We are so fond of boasting that our ancestors were great people. Even if *they* were great, seeing what we are doing now, we don't appear to belong to their lineage. Just give a thought to what we have been doing. Of what use is our saying, "I am a brahmin and ought to be worshipped by all"? Spirituality, which is what makes anyone a brahmin, has completely vanished and a tremendous inertia has overpowered us.

We have always trampled on the depressed, poorly clothed labourers. India is well-known even today because of their labour, perseverance and artistic excellence. The taxes paid by their descendants pay for the education of our children in schools and colleges even today. Do we ever pay any attention to these poor people? Do we look upon them as our own?

Does their sorrow ever touch our hearts? The present pitiable condition of India is the result of this national sin. God, who dispenses the results of karma, will definitely give us the fruits of our actions, whether we understand it or not. This is inevitable whenever there is "theft in the chamber of the mind."[8]

We glibly say that God dwells in everything and the Divine Mother manifests through all women. But in actual practice what do we do? We say, "She is a rustic," "He is a pariah," "I must bathe if I touch him," "My food will get defiled if she looks at it," "I will become impure if his shadow falls on me." If this divergence between words and thoughts is ever driven out of India, it will be only by the young people today. It is possible to do it if they now firmly assimilate in their hearts the teachings of the scriptures and work hard to eliminate this national error.

The Gita (2.56) describes another characteristic of the illumined person: "free from passion, fear and anger." Suppose I am making a special and earnest effort to get a certain thing. Now someone or something comes as a hindrance or an obstacle in the way. The feeling that is then generated in the mind is called anger (krodha). The excessive desire to possess anything is called passion (rāga) or lust (kāma). One

---

8. This phrase in Bengali expresses the dichotomy between our inner thoughts and their external expression in speech and action.

who is without lust and anger has no attachment to anything. No matter what work we do, if we do it without attachment, it will take us to the knowledge of the One. We shall see clearly that, like meditation, our daily common activities can also lead us to the knowledge of the One, which is the goal of the yogis. For this reason we should keep attachment out of our lives: everything must be done with a higher purpose in mind and we should remain calm. No work of an illumined person is done under the sway of passion and anger, which are the products of selfishness. Thus in order to attain knowledge we have to keep our senses under control, give up all selfish prayers and desires, and remain steadily focused on the ideal, unmoved by joy and sorrow.

Then extolling knowledge, Sri Krishna says:

O Partha, this is the meaning of firmly having one's being in Brahman. Once this state is reached, no more can sorrow and delusion trouble the person. Even if this experience comes at the moment of death, that person transcends death and realizes his or her immortal nature. (2.72)[9]

If you want to practise Jnana Yoga, you need to give up everything through the process of "not this," "not this." If you want to work, do so after attaining the knowledge of the One.

---

9. एषा ब्राह्मी स्थिति: पार्थ नैनां प्राप्य विमुह्यति ।
   स्थित्वाऽस्यामन्तकालेऽपि ब्रह्मनिर्वाणमृच्छति ॥

The Role of Karma Yoga in the Gita

If we are not able to give up everything for the sake of truth, then our path is Karma Yoga. We may wonder, "Everyone does work. How can that give knowledge?" That is not right. It is true, of course, that the work done for our own enjoyment—even if it is done for thousands of years—can never take us to the knowledge of the One. The knowledge of heat and cold or of joy and sorrow is not *real* knowledge; it is only ordinary knowledge common to both humans and animals. In the same way, the work done for one's own pleasure is not *real* work; this type of work is also common to both humans and animals. It only increases our bondage. For this reason we should learn the art of doing *real* work.

All of us do some kind of work. No one can live just doing nothing. In everything both animate and inanimate, there is nonstop movement produced by work. This movement goes on even in the mind and in the intellect.

No one can rest for even a moment without doing work. (3.5)[10]

All work helplessly, controlled by their own natural tendencies. Overpowered by desire, some work to fulfil their desire. Overpowered by anger,

10. न हि कश्चित् क्षणमपि जातु तिष्ठत्यकर्मकृत् ।

some work furiously under its sway. Overpowered by
greed, some chase every novelty and exhaust
themselves. Those whose hearts are full of goodness
pass their lives doing good things. In this way, work
monopolizes everything in this world. Within every
atom there is the ceaseless activity of chemical
attraction and repulsion. This too is work of a
different kind. It is just like the mind's constant
activity.

The fact that we are working does not automatically guarantee that we shall realize the One. It
becomes possible only when all work is done as yoga.
We should work in such a way that it will take us to
the knowledge of the One. The Gita says that we
must never abstain from work. We must, however, do
it wisely, so that we don't get bound by desire and
greed.

"Should we engage in activity or not?" The Gita
discusses this question more than once and in various
ways. We know that it is necessary to work; as long
as we live we must do work of some kind or other.
This is so obvious! We may wonder why Sri Krishna
discusses this question so much. There is a reason for
it. At the time the Gita was taught, philosophical
discussions had increased to an enormous degree in
India. Based on various philosophical schools, a great
many sects had arisen. Philosophical discussions had
led to a firm conclusion that the mind was finite. It
could not transcend the limitations imposed by name

and form, or by space, time and causation. The mind, it was believed, would never be able to transcend these limitations. All philosophers were in unanimous agreement regarding this finite nature of the mind. All their researches, therefore, had only one purpose in view, namely, to find out how we could go beyond the finite mind and realize the infinite truth. It was widely accepted that the only way to attain truth was to sit with a fully quiet mind, since the mind, being finite, would never be able to grasp the infinite.

This kind of thinking had attracted even ordinary people with hardly any understanding of the philosophical concepts involved. Only a person with perfect self-control could really calm the mind. But ordinary, worldly minded people gave up only their external activities. Some of them became monks, but it was only in name! In order to remove this kind of misunderstanding, Sri Krishna felt it was necessary to discuss at length whether or not it was right to remain active. That is why he made such great attempts to teach us the real nature of work, the right way to do it, and the true meaning of giving up work and being free from all bondage. It is for this reason that Sri Krishna elaborately explains the path of Karma Yoga in the third chapter—as also in many places of the fourth and fifth chapters—of the Gita.

4

Karma Yoga – I

Renunciation, the Only Path to Perfection

According to scholars in Europe and America, Indian religion or Indian philosophy speaks of only detachment. It says, "Don't care for anything in this world. Renounce, renounce." That is why, these scholars feel, a sort of melancholy or depressing tendency is found in the Hindu race, a kind of indifference or lack of enthusiasm for doing anything. Hindus have the attitude, "What's the point in doing anything in this evanescent life?" This has led to laziness and inertia.

How far these ideas are true becomes clear as soon as we study the Gita. I am not referring only Sri Krishna's repeated instruction to not stop working. We see that Krishna himself demonstrates at every moment of his life intense activity in the midst of intense rest. He does every kind of work, but within him there is extraordinary serenity. It is this state that Krishna refers to as "detachment."

The Western scholars' observation that the Hindu scriptures have made people inactive is therefore not true. Western scholars think that their

religion has made them a great warrior race and
that is why they have such worldly prosperity and
energy for work. Even that is not really accurate.
The teaching of renunciation is found in numerous
places in the Bible: "The foxes have holes and the
birds of the air have nests, but the Son of Man
hath not where to lay his head." When we read the
life of Jesus we see that it is like that of an Indian
monk. They have now twisted the meaning of the
Bible and are interpreting it according to their needs.
Does it mean that we too must accept that interpretation?

The Gita says that people practise religion
according to their nature. The Anglo-Saxon race has
both suppressed and fought with everyone because
they are filled to the brim with passion *(rajas)*. What
wonder, then, that they would understand the
essence of religion also in their own way! In reality,
however, the essence of all religions is the same.
All religions teach us that giving up is the only path
to absolute knowledge and immortality.

From the study of the *Mahabharata* and the
Gita we realize that in those days, for some reason or
other, doubts had sprung about what is work *(karma)*
and what is non-work *(akarma)*, which work is proper
and which is not, and whether knowledge—the goal
of human life—can be reached through work. That
is the reason behind the Gita's repeated teaching
that knowledge and work are not different. Work

purifies the mind and, as a result, knowledge dawns automatically.

Arjuna however is not able to follow this teaching easily; he keeps forgetting it. For this reason Sri Krishna tells him that all don't have to follow the same path: either we should do all work as a matter of duty, with no thought of self-interest, or we should give up the pursuit of desire and greed, and take up monastic life dedicated to a specific ideal. The result of following either of these paths is the same. This is because both paths teach us detachment. Total renunciation of the lower self is the only way to perfection.

Even secular work done for one's own enjoyment and pleasure gradually teaches us the value of detachment. The sage Kapila, the father of the Samkhya philosophy, says that the creation of the world is an amazing enterprise of nature *(prakṛti)* designed specifically to make the Self *(puruṣa)* realize its own glory. We realize the truth of this when we see people getting blow after blow when they try to find fulfilment through enjoyment and pleasure. Gradually, as days pass, they become fed up with the ephemeral joys and learn to give them up. Like cajoling a child to make it drink medicine, nature holds before us some ephemeral thing like fame, beauty, success or power in a way as to make us feel if we can only get that one thing, then we can have whatever we want. By this trick how easily does nature make us realize the worthlessness of all *other* evanescent things!

Suppose a particular man has the desire to become someone great. Initially he may think that being great means being rich and having several subordinates under his control. After much struggle he perhaps does become rich and his intellect also becomes somewhat refined. Then this gentleman realizes that he can be greater still if he acquires knowledge. If he is ignorant, why would people accept him as a great person? He realizes that in order to get knowledge he must learn to sacrifice a little more. He must keep himself away from partying and other forms of entertainment. In this way, to the extent that he begins to understand the meaning of being "great," he gradually realizes that no one can become great without learning to give up. In this way we all learn that nothing can be achieved in any field without giving up. The scriptures say that we learn to give up little by little in small matters and ultimately we are able to give up everything and attain immortality.

The more we advance through doing work as yoga, the more are we able to understand and accept a higher ideal of greatness. In order to attain it, we realize that we need to let go of smaller things, and so we give them up. The illustration which Swami Vivekananda gave is very apt in this context: From our planet we see the sun as a plate. Go near it by a thousand miles and how big the same sun appears! Go another thousand miles and it appears still bigger. But we know that it is the same sun. In the same way, although we may feel that we had been holding on to the same ideal all along, our idea will become higher and higher until it becomes God-realization. Sri Ramakrishna used to say that if we hold on to one subject well, we can then ultimately see in it the complete manifestation of God.

Karma Varies from Person to Person

The Gita says that, depending on the state of our evolution, we judge sense enjoyment and spirituality, active life and detached life, as worthy or unworthy, as something to be achieved or something to be rejected. In other words, some feel that the path of spirituality is right and others feel that the path of sense pleasures is right. Everyone's karma is not the same: the karma of an ordinary person is limited to his or her own enjoyment and maintenance of the family. Those who have risen to a slightly higher level think of their country. They become anxious with thoughts about how their people can have sufficient food to eat, how they can get better education, how they can keep in step with the other nations of the world. Those who have risen still higher worry about how their people can keep to the right path, become self-controlled, treat others with compassion and not become unjust and tyrannical. This is because they realize that the nation will be destroyed as soon as those evils creep in. The karma of those who have risen higher than this encompasses the whole world. Such people are immersed in contemplation on the ways to bring about the lasting welfare of people belonging to all classes, all countries and for all time. The incarnations of God *(avatāra)* belong to this category.

Sri Krishna says that the path of knowledge *(sāmkhya)* and the path of detached work *(yoga)* are not mutually contradictory. Only fools think that they are different. Sri Krishna tells Arjuna that he had not become so competent a student as to give up work altogether. He must reach his goal through doing work. Those whose minds have become totally free from all selfishness by unselfishly doing their duties attain a superconscious state through meditation. Unless Arjuna can do this, there is no point in simply working. Only those who have fully controlled their minds can cross the human boundary on the ladder of spiritual evolution. Different rules apply for those who have reached that state. Krishna tells Arjuna that he should understand this and set himself to work.

Wrong Notions about Work and Non-work

According to the scriptures, the highest result of working in a proper way is attaining the state of non-work. A misunderstanding of this idea had produced a disastrous result before Sri Krishna was born. Giving up their duties, many hypocrites, cheats and ignorant people were posing as great souls. People would turn up their noses when told of someone who was a great worker. Or they would look at such people with compassion and say, "Ah, they haven't understood yet! Well, gradually they will realize the truth. Nothing can be achieved unless one gives up work."

Everywhere and at all times people have been committing this type of blunder. Sri Chaitanya said that devotion "untainted" by knowledge is greater than devotion "combined" with knowledge. But he also said that cultivating devotion "combined" with knowledge is the only way to attain devotion "untainted" by knowledge, which is also known as unconditional devotion. Since many Vaishnavas, who are Chaitanya's followers, did not remember this, one can see their poor condition today. All of them want to instantly attain devotion "untainted" by knowledge! Whoever practises devotion in combination with knowledge is, in their opinion, doing something very wrong. Everyone wants to be great all at once. How much midnight oil has to be burnt, and what a lot of sacrifice and effort are necessary to become great! No one wants to do that.

I am reminded of a story: A person went to a monastery and said to a monk, "Revered sir, please make me your disciple." The members of the monastery asked him, "Can you really handle the responsibility? It is very difficult to be a disciple. In this monastery a disciple has to cook the food for offering in the shrine, wash vessels, fetch water, run errands for the monks, memorize the lessons given by the teacher, obey all his commands and massage his feet after dusk." The person was in a terrible fix. He thought for a while and then asked, "What does the teacher have to do?" They said, "Oh, you want to know what the teacher does? Well, he does the worship, practises meditation, teaches his disciples and gets work done through them." Then the person said, "In that case, sir, please make me a teacher right away!"

This kind of thinking is rampant in India today. Sri Ramakrishna often quoted to us this saying of the great devotee Tulasidas: "Gurus are available in millions, but it is rare to find even one disciple." It is not as if this attitude is more common among the married than among the monastics. Some think that as soon as people become monks or nuns and wear monastic robes, they are free from all duties and they become illumined immediately! No, this is not true. Sri Krishna says:

> Whoever sees non-work in work, and work in non-work, is wise. Such a person is a yogi who has done everything that needs to be done. (4: 18)[1]

---

1. कर्मण्यकर्म यः पश्येदकर्मणि च कर्म यः ।
   स बुद्धिमान् मनुष्येषु स युक्तः कृत्स्नकर्मकृत् ।

This person, as a result of directly experiencing the Self, has always and in every situation the awareness that "I am doing nothing, I am the Self" even while working. When this person notices others sitting lazily but posing themselves as spiritually illumined, he or she sees in them a lot of activity in the form of worldly thoughts. The person who has this kind of insight alone is the truly wise amongst us. He or she is a true yogi. Only such people can do work in the way it ought to be done. In these people alone—Sri Krishna is one example—do we see the unending calm of a yogi in the midst of incessant activity.

This is what happens to those who have realized the Self through either knowledge or devotion. Even while working, they are able to see themselves as different from one who is working. They are like ripe coconuts: the kernel within has been separated from the shell. Shake the coconut and hear the sound! We, in contrast, are like tender coconuts—the kernel and the shell are closely bound to one another. A blow on the shell affects the kernel too. We become "ripe" through the practice of Karma Yoga. As in a ripe coconut, our "kernel and shell" get separated. The Self gets separated from the mind, intellect, ego, sense organs and the body. It then lives blissfully in its own true nature.

Having discarded all external coverings, the Self is able to stand by itself. Not to speak of the waking state, even in sleep the illumined person sees his or her own body as if it were someone else's, as if someone else were sleeping. The poet-saint Ramprasad sang in Bengali:

> Sleep has left me, no more shall I sleep.
> In the state of Yoga, I am awake.
> Her mystic sleep, to Her have I returned
> And have put my sleep to sleep!

This is the state in which the illumined ones live: they can understand perfectly the meaning of this song. The more selfless our work is, the more our I-consciousness gradually shifts away from the body and the senses, and comes to rest in the Self. We then experience the state described in the song above.

The Utility of Karma

Another thing may be briefly mentioned here. Everywhere in the Hindu scriptures, one can see that a special effort has been made to emphasize that spiritual freedom (mukti) cannot be attained through work. Spiritual freedom is not the effect of karma. Even Sri Krishna supports this idea. What does it mean? It is important to understand the idea properly. If we don't understand this, it will be very harmful because, in that case, work may appear to be an inferior path. We may feel it has very little to do with spiritual freedom. Were that the case, there would be no incentive to do any work and there would be no faith in the power of work.

Why do the scriptures say that spiritual freedom cannot be attained through work? It is to teach us that the Self undergoes no change whatever due to work. The Self is free from decay and growth, it is without birth and death, and it is eternally blissful. Work brings about changes in the body, the mind and the sense organs. Work cleanses and polishes the equipment through which we perceive the Self and the world. As a result, our earlier defect of seeing things hazily through the mind and the intellect, which was like seeing through a mist, vanishes and we are able to see everything as it really is. Therefore the scriptures say that work produces purification of the mind (citta-śuddhi).

It is not that the Self becomes small and, because of work, it slowly begins to expand, until at last it becomes so big that it breaks through all its bonds. If this were true, it would logically follow that if one kind of work could expand the Self, some other kind of work could contract the Self. Perhaps it might contract the Self into nothingness! That is why the scriptures say that if the freedom of the Self is the effect of karma, then it would be of a limited duration. Anything that is a result of work has a beginning, middle and end. For this reason they say that the freedom is always inherent in the Self. That is the Self's real nature. Only because it has forgotten its nature does it identify itself with the body and mind, and therefore feels itself experiencing joy and sorrow.

If we ask *why* the Self made this mistake, the scriptures say, "Dear friend, that is not something to be learnt or to be taught. Let the mistake be corrected first and *then* learning or teaching becomes possible. Your mind and intellect function only *within* the domain of that 'mistake.' How then can your mind and intellect understand the cause of that mistake?" But if we ask *how* this mistake was made, the scriptures will answer, "Knowledge has been covered by ignorance and that is the cause of all this trouble." (5:15)[2] If we ask *what* the way out is, the scriptures will say, "Ah, we have found a way! Go on doing good work without paying any heed to joy or sorrow or gain or loss. That will destroy egoism, the root of ignorance."

In due time, having reached perfection in yoga, the person attains knowledge in his or her own heart. (4: 38)[3]

The scriptures tell us that if we continue to work in this way, we become perfectly desireless and then the delusion vanishes and knowledge automatically dawns in us.

---

2. अज्ञानेनावृतं ज्ञानं तेन मुह्यन्ति जन्तवः ।
3. तत्स्वयं योगसंसिद्धः कालेनात्मनि विन्दति ।

We should not think that the body and mind will stop functioning after illumination. In fact, through the grace of God they will work in a much better way. Then we shall understand when we should work and when we should stop. We shall also know the true meaning of work and the true meaning of giving it up. Then we shall acquire the capacity to work as well as *not* to work. Ordinary people don't have that capacity: they only know to work. Even for a moment they can't stop working and be truly at rest. Like a ghost, work takes possession of them and drags them everywhere. Their slavery to work entangles them so much that the thought of rest or spiritual freedom is not even present on their mental radar. They don't even have time to die!

The Art of Doing Work

We may say, "I don't agree. Don't we sit sometimes quietly without doing any work? Don't we sleep at night? At such times we are not running about engaged in work." Sri Krishna agrees that we are not running about then. But does this mean that we stop all work? Our thoughts, worries and dreams are also a kind of work. There is also another kind of activity—breathing, heartbeat and blood circulation, for example—which is continuously in progress. How then can we claim to have fully stopped work? Sri Krishna may tell us that our argument holds no water. We are slaves to work. We are totally dependent upon it. We are mistaken if we think that we are free. We are mistaken if we think that we can work when we want and not work when we don't want. We have absolutely no idea of what "rest" means. Even if we understand this a little, we have no power to get real rest. If we want to understand the true meaning of "rest," then from this day forward we must go on doing our work for work's sake, without concern for our gain or loss. Then in course of time we will realize that only this kind of work is Karma Yoga. Work has a tendency to bind us. Karma Yoga is doing work in such a way that everything we hear, speak or do frees us from our slavery to work instead of binding us to it.

Karma Yoga is simply the "art of doing work." (2.50)[4] Work can be done with such skill that we don't get entangled in it. We can then work independently with our own will. What do we need to do in order to work like that? We must not keep an eye on our own gain. Wherever there is self-interest, there is desire for results and that leads to attachment. We must work but we must also take care to see that we are not "being worked." In any case, we have to work. We have to take care of our parents. If we are married we have to maintain the family. We have a duty to the society in which we live, to the nation into which

---

4. योग: कर्मसु कौशलम् ।

we are born and to entire humanity in general. The scriptures say that we are born in this world with three debts: a debt to the gods *(deva-ṛṇa)*, a debt to the teachers *(ṛṣi-ṛṇa)* and a debt to our ancestors *(pitṛ-ṛṇa)*.[5]

Work is unavoidable. But we should, as Sri Ramakrishna said, work like a maid in the house of a rich person. She does all the work there. She also babysits the children: she is happy in their joy and sad in their suffering. But in her heart of hearts she knows that she doesn't belong to them and the family may discontinue her service at any time they wish. We too must live in the world in the same way.

Arjuna's Dilemma

In Arjuna's life, so long as he did his work like a maid, his understanding was clear. Until then his mind had not been muddled by falling into the clutches of attachment. Until then he had remained true to the high ideals of the warrior class: ideals such as loyalty to truth, administering justice by penalizing wicked and unlawful acts, developing oneself spiritually and inducing others to do likewise, giving protection to one who seeks it, forgiveness and compassion toward a weak enemy, and opposing even

---

5. These are believed to be the three native debts every individual is born with. These are to be repaid by doing prayer and meditation *(deva-yajña)*, scriptural study *(ṛṣi-yajña)* and obsequies *(pitṛ-yajña)*.

one's close friends or relatives should they do unjust or wicked acts. Arjuna thought that it was all very easy and he could always continue to work in the same manner. But powerful indeed is the power of ignorance! All of a sudden one fine day, preparations started for the terrible massacre at Kurukshetra and Arjuna faced a life-transforming test. He saw that in the course of events, he had become bound to one side in such a manner that there was no way out. Goodness, truth, justice and reason were all supporting him. Sri Krishna, his spiritual friend of infinite wisdom, was on his side.

Not on his side, however, were those whom he respected and adored from his childhood, people whom he loved and with whom he had shared the delicate sentiments of his heart. Not on his side were those from whom no one would even dream to be subjected to oppression, injustice, wickedness and atrocity. And these people were *not* only not on his side, but were also standing *against* him. Ah! In order to be true to his warrior's duties and be faithful to that high ideal, there was no other way than to kill them. Arjuna saw that the goddess of loyalty to duty wouldn't be content unless she was offered their hearts' blood. Arjuna's brave heart could not face the situation calmly. He was thrown into a terrible vortex of countless conflicting emotions which all at once flared up within him. Love brought attachment, which overpowered his awareness of right living. As a result, his intellect lost its sense of direction and it became helpless after navigating the boat in a whirlpool.

Then selfishness arose. One by one they all came—thoughts of respect and insult, anxiety and fear regarding victory and defeat—and said, "Run away, run away! This is certainly not the right way. You are on the verge of doing something wicked. Whom are you getting ready to fight? And how indeed can you face them? See before you Bhishma, who has the boon to die at his own will. Behold your teacher Drona. See Karna, equipped with the weapon which kills at one stroke and wearing the unique earrings which protect him. See before you the immortal Kripa and Asvatthama.[6] Behold Jayadratha, the king of Sindhu, proud of the boon received from his father.[7] Will you be able to overcome them? Do you want to risk your worldwide reputation for a miserable piece of land? Run away, run away! It would be better to even live on alms. Even if you win, will you really be happy in gaining the kingdom after all this killing?" Arjuna forgot that he had taken up arms for a right cause: for truth and justice.

---

6. Kripa and Asvatthama had received a boon of a long life. So their contemporaries often referred to them as "immortal."

7. Jayadratha had received a boon that whoever slew him in battle and put down his head on the earth would have his own head shattered into pieces within a moment.

Desire, the Root of all Trouble

In similar situations in life, this is what happens to us all the time. We forget the ideal and get trapped by self-interest. Sri Krishna explains this beautifully in the Gita:

> Thinking of objects, attachment to them is formed. From attachment comes longing, and from longing anger grows. From anger comes delusion, and from delusion loss of memory. From loss of memory comes the ruin of the intellect, and from that the person perishes. (2. 62-63)[8]

When we are habituated to thinking about sense objects, we take a special liking to a particular thing. Our mind is attracted to it and becomes biased in favour of it. At once there is this desire, "I want it," and we rush toward it. When there is an obstruction, we feel irritated. Irritation produces anger. Enslaved by it, we try to remove the obstruction. The result is a kind of clouding of the mind. When that happens, we forget higher values such as truthfulness and right conduct. This is called "loss of memory." In that state, we become mad to get the thing by any means, just or unjust. We forget things like our teacher's counsel, which had until then kept us away from

---

8. ध्यायतो विषयान्पुंसः सङ्गस्तेषूपजायते ।
   सङ्गात् संजायते कामः कामात् क्रोधोऽभिजायते ॥
   क्रोधाद्भवति सम्मोहः सम्मोहात्स्मृतिविभ्रमः ।
   स्मृतिभ्रंशाद् बुद्धिनाशो बुद्धिनाशात्प्रणश्यति ॥

evil and sinful acts. As a result, the intellect gets muddled and we suffer in endless ways because of our wrong actions.

Suppose some people want to earn money in order to use it for the good of their country. In the beginning this feeling is quite strong. But when money comes to their hands, they get attached to it. Gradually the greed for wealth makes them forget the purpose they started out with and their own enjoyment or wealth itself becomes their new goal in life. That is why the goal has to be kept intact. It won't do to keep an eye on one's gain. This is what Karma Yoga means. Who can practise this yoga? Only those who have control over themselves, who have their senses under control, whose goal in life is steady, and who work like masters and not like slaves. When the goal is reached they know that their work is over and they withdraw from work.

For this reason the Gita asks us to work. It says that it is better to work than not to work. But when you work, don't desire its fruits because once the desire comes, you are caught. One can see that all those who have achieved anything great in this world have all been people of self-control who held firmly to their ideal. Who are successful students? Those who hold on to the ideal without getting involved in frivolities. Who become great in this world? Who achieve greatness in religious life? Those who remain firm to the ideal. No sooner are we without any ideal than we are lost. We won't be able to do any worthy task because the intellect will be muddled. It won't know what is proper and what is not. As a result, we will end up busying ourselves with worthless things.

A question arises: "If the desire for the results of what I do leaves my mind, then how will I *want* to do anything? Is it possible to work without having any desire to achieve some specific purpose?" This is a good question. No work is possible without a goal. But why should we calculate our own gain and loss when we approach the goal? We want to consider only that.

After estimating our own self-interest, we set ourselves to work. We educate ourselves not for the sake of knowledge but to earn our living or to make a name for ourselves. We love our families and others not for *their* sake but because it makes *us* happy. If we see deeply in this way, we notice that all our work is geared toward self-pampering. It is nothing but an elaborate worship of the ego! We have one thing on our lips and another in the mind. Unless this "theft in the chamber of the mind"[9] is stopped, we won't be able to do anything worthwhile. No right path will open before our eyes.

That is why Sri Krishna says, apparently to Arjuna but really to all of us, "The desire for fruits of

9. This Bengali phrase expresses the dichotomy between our inner thoughts and their external expression in speech and action.

work is at the root of all ruin." It is this desire for fruits that has kept us tied to our ignorance and prevents us from doing our duty. It puts blinkers on our eyes so we cannot see the truth right before us. Give up the desire for fruits totally. Only if we don't keep an eye on the fruits will we be able to free ourselves from the clutches of selfishness, which is the root of ignorance and evil. Only then will we understand what real joy is. Only then will we know what true love is. Only if we don't keep an eye on the fruits will we become yogis or people full of true knowledge or devotion. All our sorrows will then vanish.

Scriptural Study and Practice Go Hand in Hand

We may study scriptures or listen to lectures. But our study and learning will be in vain if we are not able to absorb the teachings and put them into practice in our lives. If the scriptures have no bearing on our lives or if they don't become an aid in every situation of our lives, then all our study becomes useless. This is what should be learnt first everywhere, in student life or in married life or in monastic life. It is only then that scriptural knowledge will hold aloft before us the true purpose of life, raising us from wherever we may be and in whatever condition.

Swami Vivekananda used to say, "No one in India today understands the scriptures. All end up confusing their brains after learning a few words like Brahman, māyā, prakṛti etc. Ignoring the main purpose of the scriptures, they only fight over words." If the scriptures cannot help us at all times and in all conditions, then we don't have a terrible need for such scriptures. If a scripture can show the path to a monastic but not to a married person, why would the married want such a lopsided scripture? A scripture may help us only when we give up work and retire to a forest, but it may not help us in the din and bustle of the world, in the daily toil, in disease, sorrow and poverty, in the depression that follows repentance, in the revolt of the oppressed, in the cruelty on the battlefield, in lust, in anger, in joy, in the exuberance of victory, in the darkness of defeat, and finally, in the dark night of death. If the scripture cannot light the lamp of hope in such situa-tions, then weak as we are, such a scripture is useless to us.

Suppose I am a student and I have to go abroad for higher studies or for some other good purpose. If a scripture cannot help me in that situation, then what will be my condition? When we look deeply, we can see that the scriptures are not at fault. The fault lies with us. We have completely forgotten how the teachings of the scriptures have to be—and *can* be—applied in every situation of life. Having thus forgotten it, we now think that to practise true religion we must retire into solitude. Sri Krishna has a different view. On one hand, he tells Arjuna,

"You will attain nothing in religious life if you do not
fight for the cause of justice." On the other hand, he
tells people of a different temperament, like Uddhava
and others, "Give up everything, go to the
Badarikāshrama in the mountains, and meditate with
an unwavering mind. Without doing that, you will
not attain anything in religious life." It is clear
therefore that what the scriptures want to say is this:
If you really work unselfishly by giving up all fruits of
action, you will be spiritually liberated, no matter
where you are.

Sri Ramakrishna and Swami Vivekananda have
shown us through their own lives that it is possible
for a person to work with total selflessness. They did
not bicker like we do over the nonvital parts of the
scriptures. Our life should be in harmony with
scriptural teaching: only then is it possible to know
correctly the purpose of the scriptures. This is what
Sri Ramakrishna and Swami Vivekananda have
shown us. They have taught us how to apply the
knowledge of the scriptures in our daily life. We
should learn this carefully.

This is also the purpose of your Society.[10] See
that you never forget it. Never forget that you your-
selves should first clearly understand that religion
manifests itself in various forms according to the

10. This talk, like most others in this book, was given at the
Vivekananda Society, Calcutta, and the audience consisted
primarily of young men.

needs of the place, time and person. And then you have to demonstrate the truth to the world through your lives. Never forget that you have to prove that it is possible even in these days to practise the teachings of the scriptures. You have to show that whoever is able to do this is greatly benefited and strengthened in the battle of life, in whatever condition the person may be.

If the fault lay with the scriptures or if they were full of useless, outdated and one-sided teachings, they could not have helped build the lives of Sri Ramakrishna and Swami Vivekananda. Understand this well. Don't put the blame on the scriptures. Blame your own mind because it has not the capacity to see the real meaning and the true purpose of the scriptures. Blame your own education which does not allow you even to learn how to use your eyes, ears, nose and mouth.

How many amongst us know how to use our sense organs? The sense organs can perceive subtle things only when they are taught to do so. Today the goal of our education is to ensure how good a clerk one can become. It does nothing to help the child to think along original lines, to understand subtle ideas, and to make good use of one's brain and sense organs. Modern education snatches away the children's capacity even to think, making them helpless and inert. Only if the senses are strong and active can they perceive everything and only then can knowledge come. Such is the case with yogis, who have well-trained minds and powerful but obedient senses. We want to immediately experience subtle things through our untrained and unhealthy bodies and senses. Fools that we are, is it ever possible? First of all, make your senses powerful, get them under your control through training, practise for a long time, have faith and keep up the struggle—only then will it be possible for you. We won't do that, however. We'll say instead, "Our scriptures are full of trash and falsehood. Hinduism is a myth!" What greater foolishness can there be?

I had read a story in my childhood. It was entitled "The Difference between Having and Not Having Eyes." This is how the story goes: One day two men went for a walk in an open field. One of them returned disgusted having seen nothing interesting during his walk that day. But his companion returned with great joy after collecting many new herbs, examining the fertility of the land, and filling his pockets with different types of stones. Both of them had gone for a walk in the same field. The only difference was that the second man knew how to use his eyes.

Those who travelled with Swami Vivekananda know about his keen power of observation and understanding. Many a time we travelled with him in the same region and stayed in the same place. Returning from that place he would begin to tell us many things about the strange customs of the people there, their history, and so on. Hearing him we would be dumbfounded and wonder, "When did he see and hear all these things?"

The Role of Fate

The scriptures say that only one who has a strong body, powerful sense organs and a meditative mind is fit for Vedic learning. Where is such a person to be found today? We see in India such a lot of inactivity on the pretext of "fate." Do you think that it is the result of faith in God? Not at all. The chief reasons for it are weakness and inertia. It is true that unless fate or divine intervention is favourable, no work can be accomplished. But Sri Krishna says that divine intervention happens to be just one of the five causes needed to make any work a success. Along with that there must also be:

> Favourable place and time, an energetic person, powerful and trained sense organs and, with the help of these, the person's repeated efforts with fresh methods. (18. 14)[11]

The scriptures say that without divine intervention nothing can be achieved. Holding on to this idea strongly we sit tight. We refuse to notice and listen even after seeing and hearing that the scriptures

---

11. अधिष्ठानं तथा कर्ता करणं च पृथग्विधम् ।
    विविधाश्च पृथक् चेष्टा..... ॥

also say, "Be strong, don't be lazy, continue to make efforts, go on doing work." And this is because we don't possess even a little of these qualities, immersed as we are in great inertia.

There should be desire to work and along with it there should be divine intervention. Both are essential for success. It is in our hands to be energetic and active. Over the result we have no control, nor is it necessary for us to bother about it. Our concern should be to see that we have been faithful to the ideal. This is what Sri Krishna asks us to do while practising Karma Yoga.

Karma Yoga has one more goal and that is to prevent the loss of energy. Yoga is the art of doing work. It is a technique for work through which we employ just enough energy, neither less nor more. This becomes possible only if there is no desire for the result. Suppose we desire the result and the work is unsuccessful. Then how much energy we lose in mental depression! Karma Yoga says, don't fritter away your energy. Accumulate it and transform the best part of your physical energy into mental and spiritual energies. This is the teaching of Karma Yoga and of self-control. Employ only as much energy as is called for. Always see whether you have worked to the limits of your capacity. But don't break down in dismay and waste your energy over matters not under your control. Those immersed in enjoyment and seeking fruits of action always lose their energy in this way. Naturally their capacity to work also diminishes day by day. So we must always focus only on the ideal and continue to work.

Karma Yoga and Jnana Yoga Lead to the Same Goal

Who is fit to work in this way? The person who has controlled his or her mind. What happens when a person goes on working in this manner? The bonds of karma are cut asunder and gradually he or she attains perfect knowledge.

Sri Krishna exemplifies the practice of Karma Yoga in a special way. We see that although his mind and senses did an infinite amount of work, he had not the least desire for the result. Only Incarnations like him are the real teachers of the world. Their life is meant for the spread of knowledge and for teaching humanity. Study their lives and learn to work like them. Otherwise, if we don't learn to practise control, if we work with desire for its fruits, the mind will gradually become a slave of the senses, and the senses will destroy us. It won't do to be a slave of the senses. That won't help us in any way; we shall lose track of the goal. We should keep the senses and the mind under control.

Let us have a high ideal before us and keep on working. We will see that a Karma Yogi reaches through work the same state that a Jnana Yogi attains through intense detachment. Both have the same goal, but their paths are different. Although the paths are not identical so long as the two are en route, there is no difference between the two once the goal is reached.

5

Karma Yoga – II

Harmony between Jnana and Karma

According to Karma Yoga, we have got to work. We can never remain without working: so long as the body exists, some work or other must be done. It is impossible for us to give up work.

On the other hand, we read in the scriptures, "So long as we cannot give up all work, we are far away from attaining knowledge and spiritual freedom."

At casual glance, the two ideas appear to be highly contradictory. It is very difficult to harmonize the two views. In the Gita Sri Krishna offers the teaching of Karma Yoga to harmonize these two apparently conflicting views. He agrees that unless we reach the state of total non-work, we shall attain neither knowledge nor peace. But that state cannot be reached through mere physical abstinence from work. That, in fact, will only make us hypocrites. Once we reach the blessed state of non-work, our body might continue to work but every moment we shall be aware of the truth that "I am not doing any work. I am totally separate from the body and the senses." Work can be done with such skill that, as we go on working, we gradually attain that state. The central focus of Karma Yoga, therefore, is on training oneself to be non-working even while working.

The true state of non-work *(akarma)* is this: the work continues through the body and mind but we ourselves remain non-working. But if a person abstains from physical work and the mind is kept busy with worldly thoughts, that cannot be called the state of non-work. Whoever can really remain non-working, says Sri Krishna, is wise and a yogi. Only such a person can really do all work properly.

> Whoever can see himself or herself as not working even while working and know that abstaining from work due to laziness is far from non-working, is wise and a yogi. Only such a person can do all work as it should be done. (4. 18)[1]

We have to keep the body and mind working and, at the same time, know ourselves to be totally unconnected with work, thus keeping the infinite peace of a yogi constantly flowing within us. In this way every one of us will harmonize in our lives both work and knowledge. For the liberated soul this state comes as naturally as breathing. But those of us who are still on the path have to attain this state gradually with great effort and perseverance, through the joy and sorrow that is connected with different kinds of work.

---

1. कर्मण्यकर्म य: पश्येदकर्मणि च कर्म य: ।
   स बुद्धिमान् मनुष्येषु स युक्त: कत्स्नकर्मकृत् ॥

The principal aim of the first five chapters of the Gita is to establish the relation and harmony between work and knowledge. As I said earlier, at the time of Sri Krishna there was much confusion regarding the purpose of the scriptures because people failed to understand the relation between work and knowledge: they believed the two were mutually opposed and could not be practised together.

Who can say that such misconceptions regarding many matters don't exist in India even today? Take, for instance, the "blind" faith of our older people who believe that to be spiritual we should go to the forest and that helping people cannot be a spiritual practice. Or take the "clear-eyed" faith of our so-called educated youths—developed through sitting at the feet of their English gurus—that the purpose of life is to live happily and comfortably with a spouse and children. They question the ideal of giving up worldly pursuits and seeking knowledge. They say, "What kind of knowledge is that, dear sir? It's like becoming inert by ruining our brain through unnatural means!"

Instead of swallowing others' opinions, what do we see when we study the scriptures by ourselves? The older people have completely forgotten the teaching that, unless the mind and intellect are purified through work, knowledge cannot be attained. The youths today are really "scholars without studying." Sri Ramakrishna would describe their way of thinking thus: "I haven't seen that in the newspaper!" or "The English don't accept it!" So how can such people accept scriptural wisdom as the acme of human development?

The scriptures say that we should first of all study the Vedas. That gives us faith in moral values and these values are rooted in action. To live up to them, we do different types of work. While working we have varied experiences of joy and sorrow and gradually we come to know that this world is a passing show. As a result, we stop working for our own enjoyment or glorification and try instead to do work in a detached way as a matter of duty. In this way the mind and the intellect gradually become purified and we totally stop calculating our own gain and loss. This is what real "giving up" means. Once this kind of detachment produced by right thinking takes root in our lives, an intense desire to attain the eternal Reality grows in the heart and also the knowledge of Reality dawns at that very moment. Then we perceive the One in everything and in every way. Within and without, we see only the One, and nothing but the One. Once this knowledge of the One comes, it does not go away. Once the mirage is known to be the play of light over the sands, no more can it be mistaken for water.

But even after having the knowledge of the One, it is possible to work by bringing back to some extent the idea of the "many" in order to teach others or to work for some other special purpose. Sri Ramakrishna used to say, "It is like what expert singers can do. They can rise to a high scale of musical pitch and also come down again to a lower scale. They can produce sound on any pitch they wish." Thus knowers of the One are capable of working as well as not working. But try as they may, they cannot, unlike other people, view enjoyment, wealth, success and fame as the things worth attaining or as the sole purpose of life. Those who have seen a mirage and have realized that it is not really water may see the mirage again, but they will never go to it to quench their thirst. This too is just like that.

Karma Leads to Knowledge

A great confusion can arise if we don't keep in mind that work is the only means to knowledge. All kinds of work, from the lowest to the highest, help us advance toward the attainment of knowledge if we do work without calculating our own gain and loss. In India millions of people, married as well as monastics, are making the effort to attain knowledge. This is indeed very good. But ninety-nine per cent of them have not given up consideration of their own self-interest and they are busy trying to evade work as much as possible by dubbing it the product of ignorance. The result is this: work such as eating and dressing, which is done for one's own sake, continues but work such as charity, helping the poor, serving one's country—which involves the welfare of others—is given up first because it is found troublesome and difficult. Who wants to go out of the way to help others? The result, as we see, is that the country is filled to the brim with selfishness and all are on the way to ruin.

Swami Vivekananda used to say, "The people of our country could get neither spirituality nor worldly enjoyment. Getting kicked around by others, their only aim is to somehow gather a few grains of food through physical labour. And in that too some are successful, some are not." If all these people began to work in as detached a way as possible, as taught by Sri Krishna and as shown by him in every situation of his own life, for the welfare of others, for the good of the country, for the service and education of the poor and the depressed, then all such work would take them, as meditation does, toward the attainment of knowledge. In this way the nation also would not remain in such bad condition. We can see that the unselfishness of even one person can bring about the welfare of so many people. If millions in a country are ready to sacrifice their self-interest, will such a country remain in bad condition?

On the other hand, under the British influence the English-educated Indians do some desire-propelled work no doubt, but they have no understanding whatsoever about working without any desire. They simply cannot understand the real purpose of work. So they have no inclination at all to get the knowledge taught in the scriptures. They don't even realize that there is great need to make effort to get that knowledge. They fail to understand that this knowledge, inherited from our ancient sages, is our most valuable national treasure. By the crushing slavery of centuries India has lost her sciences, her wealth, prestige—everything.

What now remains with India is only the knowledge of the One, attaining which we can become free from all wants and conquer death. Every Hindu must guard this national treasure with great care. When this knowledge is destroyed, a Hindu will cease to be a Hindu, India will cease to exist, family customs and national traditions will die out, and the race will be destroyed.

The knowledge taught in the Gita is to be realized. It has to be experienced in whatever we do, be it rising, sitting, bathing, eating, or sleeping. It won't do to rest content after getting a little glimpse of that knowledge with the help of logic, reasoning or imagination. It won't do having desire and greed, which are products of ignorance, as the motivating factors in life. If we want knowledge, we must be dedicated to that quest. We must become one with knowledge. We must become mad with it. We must become intoxicated with it!

Only when the intellect becomes sensitive and pure through the practice of Karma Yoga does knowledge come. Sri Ramakrishna used to say, "God is beyond the grasp of the worldly intellect, but He can be known through the pure intellect." The only way to attain knowledge, then, is to work without desiring the results. If we are not concerned with our own gain and loss in whatever we do, slowly but surely knowledge has got to come. Work is not at fault, it never was. The fault lies in us. Our mistake is to make our own benefit the purpose of our work. Thus we are caught in our own net and have missed the path to freedom. Sri Krishna says that if a person gives up forever the hope of his or her own gain and works selflessly for a higher purpose, then

> even if such a person kills many people, he or she really kills no one. Nor is the person tainted by this action. (18. 17)[2]

"We won't be killers even if we kill hundreds and we won't die even if others kill us"—this is what we shall experience. All of us have read or heard the stories of the chaste wife and the virtuous butcher in the *Mahabharata*. But we have completely forgotten to work like these role models did; hence this degradation. That is why Sri Krishna says that we must work unceasingly and our work must be without desire. When we work, we must remain

---

2. हत्वापि स इमाँल्लोकान्न हन्ति न निबध्यते ।

non-working within. Then we will experience the serene peace of a yogi.

Intense Peace in the Midst of Intense Action

It is said that a human being is "a condensed universe." What exists in the macrocosm, also exists in the microcosm—all of it, but in a condensed manner. On the other hand, what exists in the microcosm has also its vast counterpart in the outer world. Just as within us exists the yet-to-be-realized state of non-work in the midst of work, so also in the outer world there is always present the serene peace of non-work even in the midst of continuous change and movement.

At first glance this statement may appear preposterous. Is it ever possible to see a motionless, non-working dimension in this world, which is changing in various ways every moment? The illumined philosopher says that action and non-action, movement and rest—like the other pairs of opposites, such as pleasure and pain, light and darkness—are simultaneously present in this world. We get the idea of action and movement only by comparison with their opposites, non-action and rest. Where such comparison is not possible, we cannot perceive even action and movement. Not only do we not perceive them, but what we call action and movement do not really exist there. We see continuous movement and action in the world by perceiving and comparing the different conditions of various things. But if we consider the entire world as just one entity and try to perceive movement in it, we cannot. That is the dimension of peace, rest and non-action.

Some may say, "Come on! That's just imagination." The philosopher smiles and says, "No, my friend, this is not imagination. In fact, this is the only truth." Books of both science and religion declare that the universe is one single entity. There are no two "things" but one. There are no two "energies" but one. Moreover, the "thing" and the "energy" are but the manifestations of one and the same reality. But since we always dwell on the different things in the world, we are not able to look upon the world as one integrated living entity like the human body, which is one entity composed of various limbs. In comes our limited concept of "direct perception" to confuse us. It cannot go beyond its limits and we thus think, "Where indeed is this non-action world?"

The state of non-work is always present in the Self. In the ultimate analysis the same truth is present in every object. It is present even in the universe taken as a whole. The truth of oneness is thus not a poetic fancy or false imagination like "a flower in the sky" *(ākāśa-kusuma)*.[3] The universe

3. "A flower in the sky" is one of the traditional examples in the Vedanta tradition to illustrate a purely imaginary entity that has no reality.

exists with the One as its basis. Once we are able to clearly perceive this state ever present within us, then the fleeting events like birth, old age and its ultimate end, death, also cannot frighten us. That is why Sri Krishna repeatedly gives these teachings apparently to Arjuna, but really to all of us. Sri Krishna may tell us: "Let your senses, mind and intellect be always engaged in work. But you must learn to keep yourself away from all work after realizing your true nature of non-work. O humanity! Be conscious of your own glorious nature. Arise! Realize the unaging, immortal Self and dwell in serene and steady inner peace. Don't give in to weakness and relax your efforts or else you will invite grief by eternally trying to hold on to transient things. Give up the results of action and continue working. That is true renunciation. And that is Karma Yoga as well."

Know that renunciation is the same as Karma Yoga. (6.2)[4]

Both the paths take us to the same goal.

Both renunciation and Karma Yoga lead to freedom. (5.2)[5]

Arjuna is not able to drive away the idea that knowledge is superior to work. He feels that since work ceases when knowledge arises, knowledge is the

4. यं सन्न्यासमिति प्राहुर्योगं तं विद्धि पाण्डव ।
5. सन्न्यासः कर्मयोगश्च निःश्रेयसकराषुभौ ।

real objective or goal. For that reason it is obviously superior to work. But Arjuna forgets that the knowledge which Sri Krishna has presented before him as the goal of human life is the infinite knowledge not bound by time and place. It is not the knowledge which Arjuna has in mind, the knowledge within the domain of time and space, always bound by the chain of cause and effect. We see in the fourth chapter of the Gita that Arjuna asks the same question and Sri Krishna explains the same matter to him again. But this time he tries to explain it to Arjuna in another way.

The Genesis of Karma Yoga

Reading the Gita, we can almost visualize Sri Krishna saying something like this: "O Arjuna, don't think that Karma Yoga is a new path. Like the paths of knowledge and devotion, this path too has taken people to the highest goal since very ancient times. Well-known philosopher-kings like Janaka and others have attained perfection by following this path. This is true, in particular, about the kings: I first taught Karma Yoga to the Sun. He then imparted it to his son Manu, and Manu taught it to Ikshvaku. In this way, for many generations, for the welfare of the many and for the happiness of the many, it was practised by the powerful royal families who faithfully performed their duties.

"Today that Karma Yoga is extinct. People work for their own pleasure, no one wants to work for the welfare of others. A calculating, business-like attitude has entered even into religion, not to speak of in other fields of work. To you, therefore, once again I am teaching today the ancient path of Karma Yoga.

"Attaining perfection through this path is impossible for people who are low-minded, cowards, slaves of their senses, possessed of unhealthy bodies and who have lost all zeal. But a brave heart like yours which is ever conscious of the welfare of the many, which is full of faith, wisdom and energy, can understand its liberal ideas; you will be able to firmly grasp and practise them. That is why I am teaching this to you. Whoever is always anxious about one's body being hurt, about losing wealth, prestige, success or power, even about not attaining spiritual freedom, cannot become a Karma Yogi. A Karma Yogi is a powerful, liberal-minded, brave person who can forget himself or herself completely for the cause of truth, for removing even the slightest pain of others, for the love of one's motherland, for the glory of great souls. Such a person won't raise an eyebrow even if his or her own happiness and wealth are destroyed in the process."

It is a natural tendency of the human mind to revere anything ancient. We value whatever can withstand the forces of change and remain unchanged for a long time. It is perhaps because in our heart of hearts we always have the urge to find something eternal among the transient things all around us. This urge is more intense in the hearts of the great ones than in the rest of us. Only after seeing this strong urge in the heart of the great hero Arjuna does Sri Krishna extol the history of Karma Yoga and guide him along that path.

One more thing. Only those who belonged to the warrior class—especially the kings—used to practise Karma Yoga and as a result attained the knowledge of the all-pervading Reality. It was only from them that Karma Yoga spread among the brahmins and other sections of society. Many may be surprised to hear this. Today's brahmins will particularly be surprised because they believe that only they have had the monopoly over all the scriptural knowledge of India, and it is they who have shared it with others out of compassion. There is plenty of evidence to show that this, although true in certain matters, is not true regarding everything.

We have seen Sri Krishna saying that Karma Yoga was at first known only among the kings. In the *Chāndogya Upaniṣad* we see Aruni and *Śvetaketu*, a father and his son, both brahmins, accepting the discipleship of the king Pravāhana-Jaibali. We also see five brahmins, Pracīnaśāla and others, accepting discipleship under King Aśvapati. We see them receiving instructions regarding the knowledge of the supreme Reality from those kings. In this way, the study of the scriptures shows that it is very probable that Karma Yoga and the knowledge of the Absolute were first known among the royal families.

Hearing the history of Karma Yoga, another question arose in Arjuna's mind: Sri Krishna had said that he had first taught Karma Yoga to the Sun. Arjuna thought: "How is that possible? Sri Krishna was born just the other day and the Sun was born such a long, long time ago. How could he have instructed the Sun?" In the context of this doubt, the Gita introduces the topics concerning God, His incarnations and their real nature.

Sri Krishna says, "I had given the teaching to the Sun long ago in a different form of mine. But I clearly remember that it was I who had taught him through that form, because I am an incarnation of God *(avatāra)*. My knowledge is never lost. Both of us have been, and will be, born many times in many places and have worked, and will work, for the welfare of the many. You do not remember all this. But I remember everything."

We shall discuss next time what Sri Krishna teaches about the concept of God's incarnation.

6

Knowledge and Devotion

God is the Supreme Teacher

Sri Krishna says in the Gita:

Whenever virtue declines and vice prevails, . . . I descend
forth for the establishment of true religion. (4.7-8)[1]

Whenever there is the necessity of a teacher to show
the paths of devotion and knowledge, God descends in
the form of a teacher. He is the real Teacher and it is
by following Him that the world can progress. It is He
who opens the eyes of the soul who is blinded by
ignorance and is attached to the world. In one sense,
God alone exists as this whole world. Movable and
immovable, whatever we see is but His reflection. In
another sense, it is He who exists in all living beings
as consciousness. To re-establish true religion and
peace He comes down as the World Teacher. He
comes down in a human form but is not bound by
ignorance. To us who are bound by ignorance, He

---

1. यदा यदा हि धर्मस्य ग्लानिर्भवति भारत
   अभ्युत्थानमधर्मस्या तदात्मानं सृजाम्यहम् ।
   परित्राणाय साधूनां विनाशाय च दुष्कृताम्
   धर्मसंस्थापनार्थाय सम्भवामि युगे युगे ॥

shows the true path to spiritual freedom. Though He takes different bodies at different times in history, the incarnations are not different. They are all one. It is the same God who appears in different forms according to necessity. He gives his teaching by appearing in a form called for by those times.

God has appeared in India many times and has taught us many things. That is why India was the fountain of all knowledge. Whenever it was necessary, He has lifted India up holding her by His hands. It is for this reason that even today in this downtrodden, oppressed and famine-stricken land so many heroic souls, spiritual and enterprising, are taking birth and guiding us. That is why in India we see even now more exemplars of knowledge and devotion than in other countries.

It is in the field of religion that India has advanced. Her life force is centred in religion. It is as if we are surviving only on religion. From daily activities like bathing to bigger social events like marriage, everything here is considered a part of religion. Whether we can do all these things correctly or not, there is not the slightest doubt that all our customs and traditions are geared toward making us religious. It is true that other countries have advanced in other matters. They are on the crest of the world in politics, economics, military power and other things pertaining to worldly prosperity. India's life force is centred in religion. It was on the strength of religion that India was at the top of the world at one time. There is not the least doubt that by holding on to religion alone will she rise once again in the future. As a sign of it, we see everywhere today a growing taste for the divine name, deep faith in prayer and meditation, the desire to realize God, and discussions about the harmony between knowledge and devotion.

Knowledge versus Devotion

In earlier times, at the very mention of the word "knowledge," people would imagine all sorts of things. They disapproved of those following the path of knowledge and considered them atheists. Devotees closed their ears at the mention of "I am the all-pervading Reality" (aham brahmāsmi). On the other hand, the followers of the path of knowledge looked down upon devotees as a superstitious mob. In this way, there remains a long-standing conflict between the followers of the two paths. But this conflict never existed in the leaders and teachers of these traditions.

A story is told to illustrate this: once there was a disagreement between Siva and Rama. As a result, there began an unending war between the spirits (the followers of Siva) and the monkeys (the followers of Rama). Soon there was a reconciliation between Siva and Rama and they became close friends again.

But the war between the spirits and the monkeys did not stop! Although there was never any conflict between the teachers, their followers have always been at loggerheads with one another. Today this mutual antagonism seems to be gradually decreasing. Its intensity is slowly weakening. There is a growing awareness that the different paths—of meditation, work, knowledge, and devotion—have all originated from God and by following any of these we can attain spirituality.

As I said earlier, there is no real difference between a true follower of the path of knowledge and a true follower of the path of devotion. A study of the scriptures shows us that from among those who were known to be true followers of the path of knowledge, a pure stream of devotion has flowed and made the world pure and blessed. Again, those who were recognized as true devotees have goaded us all onto the path of equanimity by spreading the light of knowledge. Is there any harmony between knowledge and devotion? If there is, where exactly is it? This is what we shall try to discuss now.

What do we see in the books of Sankaracharya, the teacher of the path of knowledge and an incarnation of Siva? After reading his hymns on Ganga, Siva, Annapurna, and Vishnu, how can we say that he was an atheist, a dry teacher of knowledge without any devotion? A study of his commentary on the *Brahma Sūtras* and his hymns on the numerous gods and goddesses shows us that there was a perfect harmony of knowledge and devotion in him. In the same way, we see a special light of nondualistic knowledge in Sri Chaitanya, the prophet of devotion. If he despised knowledge, why did he choose to receive the monastic vows from the much-respected Kesava Bharati? We do not see any conflict between the life and teachings of the teachers of both these paths.

Where then is the conflict? The conflict is in language and presentation. The conflict is due to the selfish motives of the followers. The ultimate goal of both devotion and knowledge is the same. Both are only different paths to the same goal. The goal is to destroy the worthless "unripe-I," the "I" which has bound us with desire for the world and its delights. We have to replace it with the great "ripe-I," the "I" that says, "I am God's servant" or "I am a part of Him." Devotion and knowledge are merely two ways of destroying the "unripe-I."

Devotees want to surrender everything at the lotus feet of God. The only thing they seek in life is to remember, and then to live, under all conditions and in all ways, the truth that whatever they call their own—actions and thoughts, wealth, spouse and children—are not really theirs. These belong to God. Even actions like eating, which are necessary for the upkeep of the body, are done by devotees for the service of God and not for their own sake. They live for no other reason than to serve God the beloved.

Devotees want to drown their "I-ness" in the ocean of "Thou-ness." They want to serve God in all beings after discarding forever at His lotus feet the "I" born of egoism, the "I" which says, "I am the son of so-and-so," "I am a scholar," "I am wealthy, respectable, intelligent."

In the eyes of devotees, it is God the beloved who appears as everything in the world, animate and inanimate. He is the man, He is the woman, He is the boy, He is the girl, He is the servants and the maids—everywhere are His hands, everywhere His feet and eyes. With the full awareness that the world is God's image, true devotees immerse themselves in the service of their beloved God, who is manifesting in the form of their spouses, children and others. The devotees live in order to serve. They are not attached to anything: selfishness has left them for good. They neither protest nor are troubled even at the possibility of death. Devotees attain "freedom while living" (*jīvanmukti*) by merging their own will in the supreme will of the Divine. The sage Narada expresses the characteristic of devotion in his Bhakti Sutras as: "Devotion is the intense love for God."

About devotees, Sri Krishna says in the Gita:

Four kinds of people are devoted to Me—the distressed, the enquirer, the enjoyment-seeker, and the knowledge-seeker. (7.16)[2]

---

2. चतुर्विधा भजन्ते मां जनाः सुकृतिनोऽर्जुन ।
   आर्तो जिज्ञासुरर्थार्थी ज्ञानी च भरतर्षभ ।

Those who are affected by a serious illness or difficulty or those who are totally helpless, surrender themselves to God with great intensity. This is called the devotion of the distressed.

Enquirer-devotees are those who have the following characteristics: their mind is assailed by various doubts. They are particularly eager to know whether this world has any creator and who is responsible for the constant changes occurring everywhere in this world; they no longer enjoy material comforts and sense pleasures; no sooner do they see a holy or illumined person than they rush to him or her and seek answers to their questions; they meditate in solitude in order to understand higher truths.

The third type of devotee is the enjoyment-seeker. These are people who worship God when their minds are full of some desire but have no power in them to fulfil that desire.

The fourth type is the seeker of knowledge. This devotee is the greatest of them all. Sri Krishna says:

Among them, the seekers of knowledge excel due to their constant steadfastness and devotion to the One. To them I am supremely dear and they are dear to Me. (7.17)[3]

Their minds are always united with God. Such seekers of knowledge with their one-pointed devotion are the greatest devotees. Their minds have

---

3. तेषां ज्ञानी नित्ययुक्त एकभक्तिर्विशिष्यते ।
   प्रियो हि ज्ञानिनोऽत्यर्थमहं स च मम प्रियः ॥

transcended desire, greed, and love for sensual and
material pleasures. That is why the adjective
"devoted to the One" *(eka-bhakti)* is used to describe
them. Their single-minded devotion flows ceaselessly,
like a river, toward the lotus feet of God. Its special
characteristic is beautifully illustrated in the *Devi
Gita:* the stream of one-pointed devotion, like oil
poured from one vessel into another, never stops
or wavers even when hit by the wind of worldliness.
It continues to flow without any break.

About the characteristic of an illumined person,
Sri Krishna says in the Gita:

> The great soul who has realized that everything is
> permeated by God has attained knowledge. Such people
> are very rare. (7.19)[4]

In this way, the "unripe-I" of the knowledge-seeker,
in the form of the identification with one's body, has
vanished once and for all. Such people then realize:
"I dwell both inside and outside of everyone. I am the
witness of all. It is my power that activates the mind
and the intellect. I am the witness of the three states-
waking, dream and dreamless sleep. I dwell in all
beings and all beings dwell in me." This truth is
experienced after a great deal of practice and effort.
To get this experience, it is essential to have longing
for God. It should be as intense as the longing of a
worldly person for the world or of a chaste wife for

4. वासुदेवः सर्वमिति स महात्मा सुदुर्लभः ।

her husband or of a miser for wealth. We must be attracted to God the way a drunkard is attracted to alcohol. As Sri Krishna says in the Gita (2. 62-63), thinking intensely of worldly objects results in an excessive attachment for them and gradually leads a person on the path of destruction. We need this type of "attachment" to spiritual life. When this "attachment" grows as a result of meditation on God, we progress briskly toward spiritual freedom instead of toward our ruin.

In the beginning we ordinary people are attracted by the uplifting manner of the devotees whose love for God has made their lives holy. We long to become like them. This attachment is similar to the attachment one feels for material objects. But the difference is that this attachment takes us toward God because it is directed to a higher ideal. That is why the sage Narada and other teachers have said that desire, greed, anger etc. are to be considered enemies only so long as they are provoked by worldly objects. But once their direction is changed, they themselves become aids to God-realization.

For the fulfilment of any desire, we would do well to call upon God first, because only He has the power to fulfil all our desires. We may be in the habit of praying to Him with a mind full of desires, but in the process once we fall in love with Him, then we cannot escape any more! Our love *with* desire

gradually changes to love *without* desire. Once this
desireless love takes hold of us, there is no fear of
a fall. The sage Śaṇḍilya characterizes this love in
these words: "An intense attachment to God is love—
and that is the highest devotion." The great devotee
Prahlada said once:

> O Lord, may I think of You with that strong love which
> the ignorant cherish for the things of the world, and may
> that love never cease to abide in my heart.[5]

Prahlada says, "O Lord, may I be attracted to you
with the same intensity as that of a worldly person's
attraction to the world." At first sight it looks as if
Prahlada has said something rather ordinary. But if
we think deeply we shall see its significance. Most
people cannot think of anything higher than what is
connected with the world. If we can love God the way
everyone loves their parents, friends and family, then
God-realization won't be far from us.

The Vaishnavas have therefore classified devotion into five types. They have seen that people,
depending on their temperament, feel most comfort-
able with some particular form of relationship.
In the *Mahabharata* we see that Bhishma, Uddhava,
Vidura, Arjuna, Yudhishthira and others loved Sri
Krishna even more than their own lives. But all
did not have the same type of relationship with him.

---

5. या प्रीतिरविवेकानां विषयेष्वनपायिनी ।
   त्वामनुस्मरत: सा मे हृदयान्मापसर्पतु ॥ —*Viṣṇu Purāṇa*, 1.20.17

Vidura had the attitude of a servant toward him.
Arjuna considered him a friend. Depending on their
nature and relationship, each did things in his
own way. Uddhava left for Badarikāshrama in the
Himalayas to practise spiritual disciplines after
receiving Sri Krishna's teachings. Vidura served Sri
Krishna in various ways and wandered through
many places of pilgrimage before giving up his body
after attaining nondual knowledge and the status of
a paramahamsa. Arjuna readied himself for the war
with superhuman energy after receiving the Gita's
teachings from Sri Krishna.

    The milkmaids of Vrindaban looked upon Sri
Krishna in a way all their own: By meditating on
Sri Krishna they became one with him, forgetting
their household duties, husbands, sons, daughters
and even their own bodies. One milkmaid was locked
at home by her husband. The result was that,
meditating on Sri Krishna, she became fully absorbed
in him and gave up her body in a superconscious
state *(samādhi)*. This is mentioned in the *Bhagavata*.
When we study the episode of the *rāsalīla*,[6] we can
understand the state of absorption more clearly.
During the *rāsalīla*, Sri Krishna suddenly disap-
peared. Meditating on him, the milkmaids became
so absorbed that they forgot their own identities
and did everything with the idea "I am Sri Krishna."

----

6. See *Bhagavata*, 10.29.1-10.33.26.

Devotion culminates in such a deep state of absorption that the worshipper and the worshipped become one. Radha was once asked: "How do you look upon Sri Krishna?" She replied, "I have completely forgotten that I am a woman and he is a man and my master. Unlike the love of an ordinary woman, my love toward Sri Krishna is not due to physical attraction or his qualities. My love for him wells up on its own accord without any specific reason."

We have seen that body consciousness and the "unripe-I" go away completely at the highest level of devotion. Now let us see how far this is true for the seeker of knowledge. The knowledge-seeker says that this "I" is not real; it is a product of ignorance. Where is the real "I" ? The real "I" is beyond the body, mind and everything. It is the witness of all these. It remains unchanged in all states. It neither grows nor diminishes. The real "I" dwells in all. This "unripe-I" of ours is just a part of the "ripe-I" or the real "I". The "unripe-I" comes from the real "I". The goal of the knowledge-seeker is to always remain aware of the real "I", and to merge the "unripe-I" into the real "I".

It is clear then that the devotee's state of "absorption" and the knowledge-seeker's "merger" with the real "I" are one and the same. Both the devotee and the seeker of knowledge want to drown the "unripe-I." Hanuman was once asked, "How do you meditate on Sri Rama?" He replied: "When my mind is connected with the body and senses, I see that He is my master and I am His servant. When I become aware of myself as an individual soul, I see that He is the whole and I am a part of Him. He is like the sun and I am just one of the many rays of the sun. When my mind transcends all limitations in the superconscious state, I see that He and I are one."

It is clear, therefore, that if I am identified with the body and my own interests, it is meaningless to say, "I am He" (so'ham). When I realize myself as an individual Self (jīvātman), I shall see myself as only a part of God. Freed from all bondages when I realize my true nature, I shall be one with the object of my meditation.

The concepts of duality (dvaita), qualified nonduality (viśiṣṭādvaita) and nonduality (advaita) become relevant according to the state of one's mind. That is why we find the scriptures recording all three concepts, as they are beneficial to different types of students. We have seen that the devotee wants to surrender everything at the lotus feet of God and destroy the "unripe-I." The seeker of knowledge says, "When shall I be free? When the 'I' ceases to be!" Egoism is the source of all trouble, so both the devotee and the knowledge-seeker have the same goal. Only the language they use is different. But people don't understand this. The true devotee and the true seeker of knowledge are not deluded by words. They want to experience the truth in its totality. The Uttara Gita says:

> After churning the "milk" of the four Vedas and other
> scriptures, the wise take the "butter," the essence, and
> the ordinary scholars drink only the remaining
> buttermilk.[7]

Disregarding God, who is the essence, the real goal of
the scriptures, the scholars drink the whey of mere
grandiloquence. The seeker of knowledge alone takes
the essence, the "butter." In the *Uttara Gita*, there is
one more verse regarding this: "An ass carrying a
load of sandalwood knows only the weight of the
wood, not its value."[8] This is the condition of the
proud scholar.

Unless we practise them in our daily lives, it is
immaterial whether we have heard scriptural teachings or not. The truth has to be realized. Knowledge
and devotion are to be practised in life. To make
progress, all three-knowledge, devotion and
meditation—are essential. A bird cannot fly unless it
has two wings and a tail. In the same way, without
these three—knowledge, devotion and meditation—
our progress is stalled. If the mind of a devotee is
without knowledge and the capacity to think deeply,
it rises high during the time of devotional singing
only to fall into sensual temptations when the singing
ends. It becomes impossible then to control the mind

---

7. मथित्वा चतुरो वेदान् सर्वशास्त्राणि चैव हि ।
   सारं तु योगिन: पीतास्तक्रं पिबन्ति पण्डिता: ।

8. यथा खरश्चन्दनभारवाही भारस्य वेत्ता, न तु चन्दनस्य ।

which lacks the power to think rationally. At such times, knowledge and meditation are helpful to keep one's balance. The mind must be controlled. The power to do so is within us.

Harmonizing One's Thoughts and Speech, the Principal Practice

The chief practice for this is to make our thoughts and speech agree with one another. Sri Ramakrishna used to say that real spiritual practice consists of making our thoughts and speech one. If we make our thoughts and speech the same and pray to God, won't He answer our prayer? Remember the story of Dhruva: In the forest he prayed to God after making his thoughts and speech one. There was none to help him; he didn't even have the help of a teacher. Because he had made his thoughts and speech one, God gave him a teacher and blessed him with His vision. Once we make our thoughts and speech identical, God will provide us with whatever we need. Even in the Gita, Sri Krishna tells us: "Make your thoughts and speech one."

On the battlefield, Arjuna's mind was filled with attachment and fear. There was attachment to his kith and kin who had arrayed themselves to fight at Kurukshetra. And there was also fear after seeing on the opposing side fighters like Bhishma, Karna, Drona and Jayadratha. It was not easy to fight these men. Wonderful indeed is the power of ignorance! Even a great person like Arjuna was overpowered by a temporary fit of attachment and fear. This kind of attachment and fear come naturally to all. Arjuna forgot his duty: he decided to give up the battle on account of sorrow, fear and attachment. But while he outwardly invoked religion in order to justify his desire to give up fighting and live on alms, Sri Krishna knew what was going on within his mind. Sri Krishna told him,

> You have been mourning for those who should not be mourned for. Yet you speak words of wisdom! (2.11)[9]

"You speak like a scholar or like someone who has attained supreme knowledge, but you are mourning over your kith and kin. A truly wise person does not mourn even when the body-one's own or someone else's-is being destroyed. Your words and actions are not in harmony." Sri Ramakrishna also used to tell us, "Make your thoughts and speech one." Who can stop our progress once our thoughts and speech become identical? Such is the power of this single practice that whatever we need will come of itself.

If we remember the verse I just quoted and the following verse and are able to translate them into

---

9. अशोच्यान्वशोचस्त्वं प्रज्ञावादांश्च भाषसे ।

practice, nothing more remains to be done in spiritual life.

> Give up all pursuits and take refuge in Me alone. (18.66)[10]

In other words, "Make your thoughts and speech one, and surrender yourself to Me."

See God in Everything

There is another thing that we have all forgotten, namely, seeing God in all beings. Sri Ramakrishna used to say, "Live in the world like a maid in the house of a wealthy person." The maid brings up the children of the master like her own, but knows that she'll have to leave at once when she is dismissed from her job. We must live in the world like that. God Himself has kept your spouse, children and others with you as His deposit. Not really just as a deposit, God Himself is receiving your service in and through the forms of your spouse and children and others. No matter what you do, you are only worshipping Him. You may be feeding the poor or giving a coin to a beggar, but it is He Himself who is accepting your service in the form of the poor and the beggar. Keep this idea in your mind and go on working. Give up egoism. It is only egoism that leads

---

10. सर्वधर्मान् परित्यज्य मामेकं शरणं व्रज ।

to total disaster. Once you understand this, there is no fear for you and nothing can bind you. It is my earnest prayer at the lotus feet of God that this idea may dwell always in the minds of all of us from this day forward.

Om Hari Om
Peace Peace Peace